All Contraries
Confounded

All Contraries Confounded

The Lyrical Fiction

of Virginia Woolf,

Djuna Barnes, and

Marguerite Duras

by Karen Kaivola

University of Iowa Press ꙮ Iowa City

University of Iowa Press, Iowa City 52242
Printed in the United States of America
First edition, 1991

Printed on acid-free paper

Library of Congress Cataloging-in-Publication Data

Kaivola, Karen, 1957–
    All contraries confounded: the lyrical fiction of Virginia Woolf,
    Djuna Barnes, and Marguerite Duras/by Karen Kaivola.—1st
    ed.
        p.   cm.
    Includes bibliographical references and index.
    ISBN 0-87745-323-3, ISBN 0-87745-324-1 (pbk.)
    1. Woolf, Virginia, 1882–1941—Criticism and interpretation.
    2. Barnes, Djuna—Criticism and interpretation.   3. Duras,
    Marguerite—Criticism and interpretation.   4. Fiction,
    Modern—Women authors—History and criticism.   5. Women
    and literature—History—20th century.   I. Title.
    PR6045.O72Z746   1991   90-24358
    823'.91209—dc20   CIP

Contents

Acknowledgments

I want to thank Carolyn Allen for her challenging responses to early versions of this project, her assistance in helping me shape my ideas, and her more general encouragement and support of my work. I am grateful to Evan Watkins, Katherine Cummings, and Steven Shaviro for providing insightful feedback that enabled me to consider new perspectives. My thanks to Robert Burchfield of the University of Iowa Press for his thoughtful and thorough editing. And special thanks to Malcolm Griffith, who continues to be my most careful reader and most demanding critic.

1 Introduction

In a 1989 article about Kate Chopin and Charlotte Perkins Gilman, Marianne DeKoven suggests that early female modernists' texts are permeated by ambivalence, an ambivalence rooted simultaneously in a desire for and fear of the new. The modernist moment (approximately 1890 to 1945) was a time in which a new order appeared possible, and the possibilities inherent in such change seemed simultaneously alluring and terrifying. Although ambivalence also characterizes traditional notions of modernist texts as forms which both use and transform nineteenth-century modes of representation, DeKoven extends and makes more specific this traditional characterization by suggesting that modernist ambivalence takes shape differently in male and female authored texts.[1] As DeKoven writes, the new order was "alluring to male modernists in its promise to destroy bankrupt bourgeois culture and to female modernists in its promise, simply, of freedom and autonomy; terrifying to male modernists in its threat to destroy their privileges and to female modernists in its potential for bringing on retribution from a still-empowered patriarchy" (21).

Feminist perspectives on gender, culture, and representation have brought about significant shifts in the ways we think about twentieth-century literature. DeKoven joins other feminist critics, including Sandra Gilbert, Susan Gubar, Rachel Blau DuPlessis, and Jane Marcus, in the important project of rereading modernism through the work of women writers.[2] For DeKoven, new expressions of resistance to convention become possible for female writers with the development of modernist forms capable of sustaining the most powerful kinds of ambivalence. This ambivalence is "not the dehistoricized 'paradox,' 'tension,' or 'ambiguity' of the New Criticism, resolved, contained, or unified by an organically coherent form, but a simultaneity of irresolvable contradictions" (21). These contradictions, far from weakening female resistance or resolving gender conflicts in order to reproduce conventional patriarchal ideologies, actually enable powerful opposition to a firmly entrenched male dominance. Without the "doubleness" contradictory forms make possible, resistance would have been too risky, because the threat these writers perceived was either external or internalized as repression.

DeKoven's analysis of ambivalence in Chopin's *The Awakening* is particularly compelling. She shows that although there is no ambivalence in Chopin's rejection of Edna's passivity or her marriage, Chopin is finally unable to resolve whether Edna's rebellion is a worthy struggle toward freedom and autonomy or merely the worst sort of childish self-indulgence:

> Chopin believes Edna's awakening frees her, makes her whole and autonomous, puts her in touch with the things that matter, offers her salvation from her deadened, passive married life. At the same time, Chopin believes the opposite: that Edna's awakening is not only pyrrhic, doomed, and megalomaniacal but also superficial and passive, consisting of no more than a regression to a childish state of self-indulgence, in which Edna follows every passive whim, shedding not so much false values as adult responsibilities, and ending in reckless, unconscious, but nonetheless wilful self-annihilation. In short, Chopin was just as afraid of liberation as she was eager for it. (28)

The text asserts that Edna's rebellion is both good and bad. The narrative stance shifts, producing a text that is contradictory and self-canceling, a narrative that opposes itself. This oppositional structure diffuses Edna's anger and desire while simultaneously creating the conditions for expressions of female anger and desire.

Forms of ambivalence similar to what DeKoven finds in the work of early female modernists persist throughout the century in women writers' texts and in especially pronounced ways in the lyrical novels of Virginia Woolf, Djuna Barnes, and Marguerite Duras. Ambivalence characterizes and shapes the feminist politics of all three writers, for each represents female experiences of being at once "within" and "without" ideology. That is to say, they resist and support an oppressive patriarchal status quo. In emphasizing this doubleness—the condition of being within and without ideology and its representations—these writers produce a distinctive form of ambivalence. In the modernisms of Virginia Woolf and Djuna Barnes and in the postmodernism of Marguerite Duras, ambivalence is often a response to what—for complex reasons—these writers feel should not be said explicitly. Their work charts boundaries between what is socially sanctioned and what is forbidden. And Duras's work further complicates these boundaries by showing language's mimetic failure. These authors both reveal and conceal their subjects—and Duras goes further to suggest the failure of representation to reflect experience and subjectivity as they exist in the world.

In a figurative sense, these writers rework one of Western culture's first paradigmatic narrative forms, the mystery and subsequent revelation of incest in the story of Oedipus. Traditional narratives follow the form of the Oedipal story as a representation of transgression but also of resolution and recuperation. They reassert the imperative of maintaining codes essential to the reproduction of existing society. If traditional narratives follow the shape of the Oedipal story, enacting the necessity and the power of society and law, Woolf, Barnes, and Duras develop structures that question and subvert existing social codes, for their narratives depict transgressions but do not resolve these transgressions. Their narratives do not end with recuperation or resolution but remain open and unsettled. However, they suggest that certain breaches of the social contract, certain transgressions as seen and experienced from female perspectives, must remain disguised, hidden, and displaced. The reproduction of existing social structures in patriarchal cultures depends upon women's participation in their own subjection— women's participation is essential to the reproduction of conditions that create their own oppression and vulnerability. Patriarchal culture must produce female subjects who internalize the necessity of remaining silent about their victimization and oppression at all levels—from the ways women internalize these values to their experiences in families, couples, and society. Thus, the decision to speak rather than remain silent involves risk and ambivalence. One never knows in advance precisely what will result from the decision to represent one's experience in a way that departs from the dominant culture's normative representation. For example, Woolf writes from her own place and time that it would be impossible for a woman to write the truth about her body and its passions because men would be shocked. And Woolf did not speak publicly, at least not for a very long time and then only to close friends, about the ways she was sexually abused by her half brothers, Gerald and George Duckworth.

The ways all three writers both record and obscure female experiences of incest illustrate the complications that result when a woman decides to represent her experience and remains acutely aware of the vulnerable position in which she is placed by this decision. At least in the fiction, incest is concealed even as it is revealed. Woolf wrote in her memoirs of how she was sexually abused by her half brothers, but in her fiction she never wrote explicitly of it or incest more generally, although incest is suggested in *Between the Acts*.[3] And when Barnes wrote of incest in *Nightwood*, she distanced it from herself by making it part of Nora's dreamworld and displacing it onto the grandmother.[4] Duras, in her most autobiographical text, *The Lover*, suggests the possibility of incest, however obscurely.[5] This is not to insist upon a link between actual incestuous experiences in these writers' lives and the ambivalent structure of their fiction. Rather, for a variety of complex reasons having to do with female experiences in a male-dominated public world, these writers developed strategies that enabled them to reveal and conceal their subjects. This doubleness has much to do with fiction that is about what women cannot or are not supposed to say. And, of course, incest is just one of many forbidden subjects.

Female vulnerability in the world provides a useful way to understand writing that both reveals and conceals, especially writing that also subverts normative notions of sexuality, desire, anger, and aggression in order to write about female experiences differently. To make trouble by representing what the dominant culture doesn't want represented—such as female experiences of incest or anger at women's subordinate status and limited opportunities—is to risk some form of punishment that may involve being labeled in undesirable ways or being ostracized from one's family and community. Woolf represents female vulnerability in *Between the Acts*, for, although the women in Bart Oliver's house are not physically attacked, the male threat is always present. In the newspaper account of the rape Isa reads and then immediately represses until the end of the text, a woman is brutally attacked by soldiers. Isa is surrounded by men who ostensibly protect her from the terrors of the world at large, but Woolf makes clear that these protectors could quite easily become attackers. Bart Oliver, the patriarchal head of the household, is not just a military man (like the soldiers who do the raping in the article), he is gruff, brutal, and controlling. He terrorizes his grandson and, when the boy bursts into tears, rejects him for not being "manly." Similarly, his son Giles Oliver (Isa's husband) crushes a snake swallowing a frog, violently destroying what displeases him. The women in this text, "protected" within the patriarchal household by these men, are vulnerable indeed. In fact, a woman is said to have drowned herself on the grounds. The submerged image of the drowned woman haunts the text, but is not acknowledged by the Olivers, only by the servants. And the femininity the men approve, the femininity of a Mrs. Manresa, is the artifice of a male-defined female sexuality. Mrs. Manresa exists merely as an object for male pleasure; she has no more power than the other women. To adopt unthinkingly this masquerade of femininity is not to guarantee one's safety—for Mrs. Manresa is as dependent as the other women on male benevolence—but, Woolf suggests, it is instead to lose one's sense of self. What female desire or sexuality might look like from "elsewhere," from beyond this male definition, remains a mystery.

Woolf, more than Barnes or Duras, felt it would be impossible for her as a woman to write beyond the culturally legitimate territories of female sexuality as defined by men into the more dangerous and transgressive—and previously unwritten—ways women actually experience sexuality, desire, pleasure, and power. She describes her own struggle with these internalized boundaries as inseparable from her gender. The rhythm and repetition of a lyrical prose style are for her, as for Lily Briscoe in *To the Lighthouse*, ways to resist circumscription and the containment of consciousness. Woolf experiments most fully with the possibilities of rhythm and repetition in *The Waves*. But her last novel, *Between the Acts*, reflects Woolf's own sense of her literary accomplishments as limited: there is a new story to tell, a story of women's experiences that will break with established codes much more fully than she felt she was able to accomplish in her own fiction. This hitherto unwritten story will undo history in order to dissolve the barriers between the intelligible and the irrational, barriers separating "Man the Master from the Brute" (184), and to articulate the "unheard rhythm of [our] own wild hearts" (65). The difficulty of breaking through internalized barriers was, for Woolf, profound.

Djuna Barnes's *Nightwood* explores more explicitly the implications of this "unheard rhythm." At the end of *Nightwood* it is literally true that the barriers between humans and beasts have broken down: Robin, engaging in a strange ritual with Nora's dog, goes down on all fours in the chapel. In terror, the dog retreats to the corner as Robin approaches relentlessly, "grinning and whimpering" (170). As perverse or troubling as this scene may be, there is, we are told, in Robin's barking something "touching" as well. Her anguish is complete and consuming, and the agony in this final scene propels us into the void Matthew prophesizes: "Now . . . the end—mark my words—now *nothing, but wrath and weeping!*" (166). It is indeed "nothing," for as an ending it resists resolution: it does not serve but rather challenges the interests or reproduction of conventional social forms.

Barnes extends this project of writing toward forbidden subjects and what is unknown, given the cultural factors curtailing women's expression, by weaving together gender and sexuality with desire, violence, and pain. By moving beyond purity, she fractures cultural definitions of femininity. But this willingness and ability to transgress do not mean that Barnes was able to produce, as one might assume, a more liberated female subject; instead, her representations of sexuality, obsession, and violence show how subjects marginal to or outside the dominant culture internalize its forms in ways that lead them to become painfully in collusion with what is, logically, in their best interests to resist or undermine. In short, the women in *Nightwood* are as contradictory as the text itself. *Nightwood*, while insisting on the centrality of history, tries to escape history: as a critique of the dominant culture, *Nightwood* grounds itself historically in order to strengthen its resistance to oppression. But Barnes's theatrical, performative, spectacular prose also embodies a desire to be free of the confines of society.

Marguerite Duras resists the social order in ways more abstract and symbolic. By producing representations that seem, paradoxically, since they are constructed in language, largely uncontained by language and that demonstrate the limits of language, she questions the ability of language to adequately symbolize and structure experience. She accomplishes this in part by using a mesmerizing cadence to threaten intelligibility and challenge representations of coherent, stable individuals in control of their emotions, desires, and actions. The former results in writing that challenges its own premises. The latter produces figures who are not motivated in the way traditional fictional characters are and whose actions and impulses are unchecked and often indecipherable.

Duras insists explicitly on complexity and contradiction: "If writing isn't, all things, all contraries confounded . . . it's nothing. . . . if it's not, each time, all things confounded into one through some inexpressible essence, then writing is nothing but advertisement" (8). This passage from *The Lover* describes her fiction well, for her writing blurs distinctions, questions boundaries, and confounds contraries. In fact, the passage cited illustrates its claim: the text heightens our awareness that these ideas about writing are spoken not by Duras but by a fictional persona who often appears inseparable from her in the text. The photographs of Duras on the front and back of the book seem, given the way the speaker describes herself, to represent not Duras but the fictional speaker herself. But the speaker cannot *be* Duras, and the photographs therefore are not of her, for the speaker "remembers" fictional figures from Duras's oeuvre as if they were real people from the speaker's own childhood. What results is an intertextuality that calls attention to the way Duras blurs distinctions between fiction and autobiography, writing and experience.

Of these three writers, Duras connects writing itself most explicitly with domination and violence. Desire, eroticism, sexuality, and subjectivity become inexorably linked with violence, domination, and writing. In Duras's texts, writing does not coincide absolutely with experience, but experience is never entirely out of relation to writing and representation. Writing shapes subjectivity, but the body—however much inscribed by culture—always exceeds representation and therefore becomes a powerful subversive force. And yet writing also lacks authority: Duras refuses to grant writing an unambivalent, noncontradictory kind of power. To some extent, then, she deconstructs the authority of her own position in discourse, which, in the context of recent poststructuralist theory, raises troubling questions for women about the effects of having no fixed position in discourse, since it is more important to construct positions for women than to take away what women have never had.

Instead of attempting to resolve the antithetical oppositions that

riddle their texts, all three writers put oppositions into moving contours of struggle that remain unresolved. In so doing, they resist
and subvert impulses to label, categorize, and marginalize. They
resist the will to control or abolish difference, and they refuse structures of containment and purification. Pleasure merges with pain,
love with hate, eroticism with violence, sense with unintelligibility.
The result is the imbrication of pleasure, desire, eroticism, sexuality, and violence in contradictory portrayals of female subjectivity.
In these portrayals, the authors resist and subvert normative cultural representations by writing female subjectivity differently, but
they also remain complicit with dominant ideology.

Complicity is not, of course, full affirmation or strict adherence.
It is rather an awareness of difference and contradiction, of being
both inside and outside ideology and its cultural representations.
Inside ideology we are necessarily complicit in its reproduction;
outside we are able to resist and subvert ideology and its representations. Louis Althusser claims that ideology is "not the system of
the real relations which govern the existence of individuals, but
the imaginary relation of those individuals to the real relations in
which they live" (165). Being completely inside ideology, Althusser's subjects believe they are completely free of ideology. Yet, as
Teresa De Lauretis has argued, women as historical subjects are
caught in an irreconcilable contradiction: women are "both inside
and outside gender, at once within and without representation"
(*Technologies* 10). This contradiction is the basis for feminist theory. Although women are caught in gender as Althusser's subjects
are caught in ideology, we know that we are not equivalent or re-
ducible to cultural representations of gender. But we are governed
by very real social relations, and these relations obviously include
gender. Moreover, and importantly, De Lauretis notes that "to what
extent this newer or emerging consciousness of complicity acts
with or against the consciousness of oppression . . . is a question
central to the understanding of ideology in these postmodern and
postcolonial times" (*Technologies* 11).[6]

Because the fiction of Woolf, Barnes, and Duras subverts but also
remains complicit with forms of oppression, it is an unusually powerful place to pursue an investigation of how "complicity acts with
or against the consciousness of oppression." While the politics in
these texts is often explicitly feminist, the texts themselves are
deeply equivocal. This equivocation makes for provocative writing,

but it coexists uneasily with feminism, for feminism is not ambivalent or equivocal: its politics of resistance to male privilege and domination is unambiguous. Still, these texts are of particular interest to feminists precisely because they represent female subjectivity in contradictory ways that help us understand how it is constructed in the world.

If these texts occupy a problematic position in relation to feminism, they are equally problematic in relation to other political positions rooted in a commitment to social change. For instance, because these texts emphasize the private and individual over the public and social, they to some extent replay what Frank Lentricchia notes in his study of Wallace Stevens in *Ariel and the Police* is a classic contradiction of the middle class, which he characterizes as

> on the one hand, our retreat to the interior, whether of our homes, our families, or our writing—wherein we indulge the sentiment that our private life is our authentic life—and our concurrent disavowal of all possibility for happiness in the public sphere, or in relationships not sanctioned by the public sphere; a retreat, a disavowal, on the other hand, incessantly accompanied by an incipiently explosive dissatisfaction with all private (and aestheticizing) solutions to pains whose sources are not personal and which require keen attention to history's plots. (207)

Stevens's writing retreats to the interior, for it explores internal, private experiences and makes subjective experiences the most authentic. But while Lentricchia can convincingly claim that Stevens does not analyze the public world or pay "keen attention to history's plots," the same argument cannot be made so easily with Woolf, Barnes, or Duras. They do not ignore historical and cultural contexts, and they show how the personal and the public are intertwined. And yet, as in Stevens's poetry, a lyrical impulse characterizes their texts that both is and is not subversive.[7]

Lentricchia finds in Stevens an "obsessive force . . . determined by equally decisive experiences of the literary avant-garde and the decadent edge of consumer capitalism" (208). Even though the avant-garde defines itself against normative assumptions and dominant ideologies, of which consumer capitalism is certainly one of the strongest operating in contemporary society, these seemingly contrary experiences are not necessarily opposed. For Lentricchia, Stevens undoes the conventional modernist opposition between aesthetics and economics because he "not only prized the new as the different, the rare, and the strange, but could and did find triggering releases of pleasure equally in original poems and in exotic fruits at a specialty market for gourmet shoppers" (208). (Interestingly enough, since Lentricchia attempts to break down gender dichotomies in his discussion of Stevens, his own discourse inscribes a masculine bias: "triggering releases of pleasure" linguistically weaves together guns, violence, and male sexuality.) The two delights converge, though one stems from the pleasure of the text, from linguistic riot, and the other from a sensuous perception and pleasure in surfaces. Both desires are produced by consumer capitalism: the capitalist subject, male or female, is a desiring subject who continually demands the new and the different. In this sense, the function of the pleasures may not be so different or, in the case of literary texts, so subversive. Ariel, the spirit of imagination and fantasy, is a potentially powerful subversive force but in fact serves more conservative ends, providing pleasurable diversion from material conditions. As a result, the two pleasures seem more complementary than contradictory.

For Stevens, the aesthetic moment is isolated, purified, and withdrawn from the social and is liberated from didacticism or political translation. It is distinct from the rational as well. In "Notes toward a Supreme Fiction," Stevens voices the longing for the irrational:

> The difficultest rigor is forthwith,
> On the image of what we see, to catch from that
> Irrational moment its unreason.

To catch this "unreason" requires rigor: where reason dominates, the hardest thing, Stevens suggests, is to escape what it contains and controls. But what, after all, does it mean to escape reason in a world already much too irrational and violent? In Ariel's realm, perhaps nothing serious can happen. If this is so, then, as Daniel Albright notes, Ariel is "simply a disengaged, dispassionate, almost contentless creativity, an imagination so engrossed in the continual play of images that it cannot be bothered to attend to the real" (2). To escape reason can seem, therefore, given pervasive violence in the world, potentially threatening as well as liberating.

Like Stevens, Woolf, Barnes, and Duras value the irrational, what cannot be pinned down, what is not prepackaged. And they value it because it is one means to escape the totalizing impulses that cross both social and symbolic fields. They embody a longing that often seems capable of overwhelming everything else (character, plot, narrative) in the text. It is a lyrical desire, and it is often unusually beautiful and compelling. Unlike Stevens, however, they do not go so far toward making the aesthetic moment isolated, purified, and withdrawn from the world. Ariel lives in these texts but with qualified powers. None of these writers allows the allure of her writing to remain entirely removed from the world and its political struggles, and each remains conscious of female vulnerability. If at times the lyricality of their writing becomes as seductive and fascinating as the desired female object in traditional literature, they achieve more than aesthetic pleasure by insisting on a new model of representation that is not disengaged from the imperatives of material conditions.

As an embodiment of an urge for liberation from social and symbolic conventions, lyrical writing provides a form capable of articulating structures oppressive to women (though lyricism doesn't necessarily do this and isn't necessary in order to do it), while it also expresses an impossible longing to escape these structures entirely. In the fiction of Woolf, Barnes, and Duras, lyricism complements and enhances the subversiveness of these writers' representations of female subjectivity and desire. The attempt to write female desire and sexuality into representation is a subversive gesture; it is an attempt to refute the equation of femininity with purity, which works to reinforce oppressive social structures. As Maria-Antonietta Macciocchi has argued, "the body of fascist discourse is rigorously chaste, pure, virginal. Its central aim is the death of sexuality" (75). By writing sexuality and desire into their fiction, these women resist the purity of more exclusionary and fascistic forms of discourse. Similarly, in contrast to the linear imperatives of plot, the lyrical moment is plotless; it precedes design and control. For this reason, when combined with narrative it provides an opportunity for female experiences of subjectivity and of the world to be explored or imagined.

By fracturing conventional narrative, these writers challenge rather than reinforce normative cultural patterns and the ideological positions these patterns support. As Roland Barthes and others have shown, literary texts inscribe complex cultural codes and serve ideological ends,[8] and, as Rachel Blau DuPlessis has argued in *Writing beyond the Ending*, narrative outcomes are sites where cultural assumptions are most emphatically played out and made visible.[9] DuPlessis points out that nineteenth-century novels ending with death or marriage show the characters' ability or failure to negotiate sexuality and society. Such texts, like the Oedipal narrative, implicitly reinforce cultural values by showing how one participates in the reproduction of society or is excluded from it: they demonstrate how high the price of exclusion can be. Woolf, Barnes, and Duras do not reinscribe narrative patterns that contain and purify women in this way. They produce, instead, open forms that do not resolve the problems introduced, problems that destabilize the status quo. Perhaps, as DuPlessis suggests, the open, unresolved form is the only one appropriate to a culture in radical transition, where shared cultural assumptions have broken down. The terms of sexuality and kinship are resisted, reimagined, and renegotiated in both the form and content of this fiction. While the lyrical forms of these texts are ambivalent, this ambivalence is mirrored even more emphatically in what these writers represent about female experience.

If these texts subvert the shared values inscribed by much nineteenth-century fiction and still operative today, it does not follow, as is sometimes claimed, that they subvert forms of cultural hegemony in unproblematic, straightforward ways. And yet radical, even apocalyptic claims tend to be made about literature that does not simply replicate conventional forms.

In *Revolution in Poetic Language*, for example, Julia Kristeva questions the extent to which poetic language can serve a revolutionary function in society.[10] She argues that a certain kind of literature—exemplified by such writers as Lautreamont, Mallarmé, Joyce, and Artaud—represents a new social and ideological situation in which the "capitalist mode of production produces and marginalizes, but simultaneously exploits for its own regeneration, one of the most spectacular shatterings of discourse" (15). Kristeva, who in this text is concerned with literature by male writers, questions whether literature written in language that fractures its own authority as a meaningful symbolic construct can subvert the interests of the powerful groups it critiques or whether, being produced and marginalized by patriarchal, racist, and capitalist societies, it in some way *serves* the interests of the powerful. Such a shattering of discourse is in this century concomitant with an increasingly sophisticated consumer capitalist society. Therefore, as Kristeva suggests, in highly developed forms capitalism can tolerate, perhaps even encourage, the "manifestation of the signifying process in its 'poetic' or 'esoteric' form" (16). That is to say, it can tolerate writing that foregrounds its own signifying properties and its status as representation that is not coincident with any referent. It can tolerate a crisis in linguistics because power is firmly in place elsewhere. Linguistic riot may even serve as an escape valve for pressure—such fiction allows one to experience, with minimal risk, a kind of freedom unavailable in other areas.[11]

The particular force of these writers comes not, or not solely, from their attempts to resist and subvert existing discourses and linguistic strategies. It comes rather from the complex combination of this resistance with a strong desire—a desire that has much to do with their experiences as women in the world—to retreat from political exigencies with an aestheticizing prose. Such prose produces sensuous pleasure in Woolf's fiction, a compelling obsession in Barnes's *Nightwood*, and a painful longing for which there is no fulfillment (but which is nevertheless a strange kind of pleasure) in Duras's texts. Thus, at least in part, their work plays a contradictory role in contemporary culture: it subverts and yet it remains something like the "harmless bonus" Kristeva suggests such writing may in fact be. What keeps it from being entirely harmless is the strong critique of the ways existing society effects subjectivity that informs these texts. Produced within social, political, and cultural contexts that can tolerate a plurality of voices and stances without significant threat to the status quo, their writing can resist but not significantly challenge those contexts.

At least in part this study responds to forms of feminist critical theory and practice which, in the important work of identifying and analyzing oppressive cultural structures and representations, result in unambivalent celebrations of or apocalyptic claims about women's writing. For, as inspiring as such theories and the critical practices informed by them can be, and however valuable their corrections of widespread cultural blind spots toward women's writing, such theories have, like all others, their own blind spots. One of these, at least with respect to the women writers I discuss here, is the inability to address fully the ambivalence and lines of contradiction that run through the texts of these women writers.

By focusing on the ambivalence and contradiction that mark these writers' work, in addition to their subversion of and resistance to dominant ideologies of sexism and heterosexism, I do not intend to fault them for somehow falling short of an ideal mark, for not being as radical or as liberatory as I think they should be. The implication of this study is not that women writers, particularly those who define themselves as feminists or are otherwise committed to social change, should police their work for traces of contradiction or collusion with oppressive social structures. To argue this would be to insist that women's writing be exclusively utopian and not represent or embody the contradictions and ambivalences that do in fact riddle the lives of real women in the world. Instead, I'm convinced that feminism is well served by texts that represent the contradictory ways female subjects are produced in culture and the ways in which we might be in collusion with oppressive social structures.[12] In the context of the material and social conditions of twentieth-century women, texts such as the ones I discuss in this study are in fact cultural sites where we can interrogate and thus more fully understand the contradictory ways our own subjectivities are constructed with respect to gender, ethnicity, and class. These texts also make it possible to examine the complex combinations of desire, loss, sexuality, and violence in our own lives.

What this study implies, then, is not that women should not write contradictory texts but that feminist practices must be able to account for when and how texts and representations are contradictory, for in this way we will also know ourselves more complexly and be able to analyze our forms of resistance more effectively. Texts that resist some forms of dominant ideologies are not completely outside the structuring powers of their contexts. And within the larger cultural context, texts that subvert traditional narrative forms can be alluring and seductive, particularly to feminist readers and critics who recognize the exigencies for social change. Such texts seem, especially in relation to other texts that replicate overtly and unselfconsciously existing and oppressive cultural paradigms, inspiring, liberating, and even harbingers of a different kind of material future. In their resistance we see new representations, new

Ambivalence & Contradictions

forms for new experiences and subjectivities. But effective resistance requires clear and precise analyses, not wishful thinking, which is why it is imperative that we examine critically cultural texts and our responses to them without repressing consciously the truth of our responses—even when we fear these responses fail to correspond to intellectual positions to which we are committed.

Although it is true that these writers subvert conventions of narrative and representation and discourses of mastery and domination, their work is unexpectedly ambivalent and contradictory. It thus resists assimilation to critical practices that make subversiveness or heterogeneity an unproblematic celebration of what is professed to be a space uninscribed by cultural forms or values. It is this ambivalence and contradiction that I explore and attempt to account for with an alternative form of feminist critical practice. This practice does not so much oppose celebratory forms of feminist theory (indeed, my debts to these theories should be clear in what follows) as it seeks to make them more complex and problematic in order to advance the work of feminist criticism as effective cultural intervention. To the extent that I use these writers' work to question the ability of existing forms of feminist critical theory to recognize and address contradiction, ambivalence, and conflict in writing by women, I focus on specific textual details and give readings of particular passages. I do this in an attempt to resist, as I believe these texts resist, the totalizing impulses of theory. And by resisting the tendency of theory to subordinate texts to its own primacy, I refuse to imagine my own critical readings of the novels as free from the ambivalences and contradictions they register; there's a sense in which my work, in relation to the previous criticism, parallels these writers' relationships to previous literary texts.

Writing that is ambivalent and contradictory insists on its own doubleness. In a double gesture, it denies itself, for whatever it asserts it also undermines. In the fiction of the women writers I discuss here—Virginia Woolf, Djuna Barnes, and Marguerite Duras—ambivalence characterizes both how they write and what they represent. It characterizes how they write because their lyricism, which distinguishes them from other twentieth-century women writers, embodies subversive urges to escape conventional novelistic forms, but these subversive tendencies can also be read as lyrical retreats into diffuse, private, individual pleasures rather than as direct resistance to tradition, whether literary or political. And, perhaps even more emphatically, ambivalence characterizes what they represent because these texts show subjectivities that resist conventional and normalizing ideologies but nevertheless remain shaped by them.

2 The Lyrical Body in Virginia Woolf's Fiction

The fact that critics have made strong cases to support divergent and even contradictory readings of the politics of Virginia Woolf's fiction shows the extent to which her fiction records ambivalence. Even as most of her fiction challenges the distribution and workings of power in society, it also invites a retreat from politics into a world of aesthetic and individual pleasure. The lyrical rhythms, random associative fragments, and sensory quality of her images produce texts more pleasurable and sensuous than critical or didactic. Woolf's lyrical fiction entices, but it does not necessarily incite a reader to greater political or social consciousness. I do not mean to suggest that lyrical, associative writing is always apolitical: many modern poets' work demonstrates quite the contrary (take, for example, the poetry of Adrienne Rich).[1] Rather, I want to emphasize that Woolf's writing both produces political and social critiques and obscures these critiques.

Because Woolf's fiction is ambivalent in this way, it lends itself to the ongoing debate about the relationship between art and politics. It also lends itself to very different feminist interpretations. For instance, in *A Literature of Their Own*, Elaine Showalter argues that Woolf's lyricism is symbolic of her withdrawal from the world, her almost "uterine" self-containment. According to this view, which is removed from the bulk of feminist criticism of Woolf (but not from much of the nonfeminist criticism), Woolf is like Bernard when he says, "I must make phrases and phrases and so interpose something hard between myself and the stare of housemaids, the stare of clocks, staring faces, indifferent faces" (*The Waves* 30). That is to say, Woolf's writing not only shapes experience but protects the self from a hostile world. Showalter maintains that Woolf's writing signals a withdrawal from the world and functions as "an extension of her view of woman's social role: receptivity to the point of self-destruction, creative synthesis to the point of exhaustion and sterility" (296). Like Clarissa Dalloway and Mrs. Ramsey, who are acutely aware of and responsive to others, the writing absorbs and smoothes over conflict and difference. And if the writing absorbs conflict and difference, it carries out a certain kind of ideological work by diverting the reader's attention away from what is radical and subversive. For Showalter, the power of Woolf's prose is paradoxical in that there is "female sexual power in the *passivity* of her writing: it is insatiable" (296). Characterizations of Woolf as withdrawn, writing about the intricacies and passivity of female consciousness, are exaggerated and false, however, when they suggest that this passivity is the only significant story to tell about Woolf's writing. To focus on it to the exclusion of other aspects of these texts presents a skewed idea of Woolf's life and art.[2]

As Jane Marcus has shown, Woolf's writing does not preclude radical politics. In addition to the fact (itself significant and subversive) that she, as a woman, wrote at all—and not only novels but essays and criticism—Woolf's redefinition of subjectivity and rejection of traditional narrative structures are political and subversive acts. Her writing challenges the deepest convictions of a society she found imperialistic and patriarchal. Writing was one way to challenge that society; as Marcus argues, "Like Kafka [Woolf] felt that writing was a conspiracy against the state, an act of aggression against the powerful, the willful breaking of the treaty of silence the oppressed had made with their masters to ensure survival" ("Thinking Back" 73). For Marcus, anger fuels Woolf's creativity, despite Woolf's conviction that women and other oppressed or marginalized people must keep their anger—however justifiable—out of their art. In "Liberty, Sorority, Misogyny," Marcus points out that *Between the Acts* "tells us that 'what we must remember' is the rape; 'what we must forget' is the male rewriting of women's history" (76). But what Marcus must herself "forget" in order to construct such an unambivalent argument is Woolf's insistence that art and polemic be distinct, her various struggles to negotiate between art and politics in novels that span more than twenty years, and her own internalization of what Marcus calls the "treaty of silence" that ensures the survival of the oppressed. Nor does Marcus distinguish between the different ways the novels and the essays treat the contradictory claims of art and politics.[3] In viewing Woolf as a socialist feminist whose work critiques the material conditions of women's lives, Marcus obscures the intense ambivalence so central to Woolf's work. Moreover, while Woolf's awareness of social conditions is indeed central to her thinking, she also suggests that if certain social and economic constraints were removed, the artist would be able to create *freely*, without limitation. This belief implies an idealist view of subjectivity quite at odds with materialist frameworks. According to Michelle Barrett, Woolf's socialist argument cannot be construed as a Marxist argument because she "explores the extent to which, under adverse conditions, art may be restrained and divorced from social conditions, but retains the notion that in the correct conditions art may be totally divorced from economic, political, or ideological constraints" (23). While critiquing the idealism of liberal humanism, Woolf embraces its underlying assumptions.

Marcus and Showalter made these arguments over a decade ago, but critics still debate the uneasy relationship between Woolf's art and politics, suggesting that the questions raised then are far from resolved.[4] Barrett describes this uneasy relationship quite well: "It would be wrong to argue that Virginia Woolf ever subordinated her conception of the integrity of *Art* to the overt expression of her political views, and indeed there is a real tension in her work between the two. While much of her work is explicitly political in nature, and of course *Three Guineas* is highly polemical, [Woolf] frequently resisted the intrusion of any attitude which, as she wrote to Lytton Strachey, 'gets into the ink and blisters the paper' of her novels" (22). For the most part, however, feminist critics read Woolf as less ambivalent, emphasizing, as Marcus does, the radical and subversive aspects of her work. And yet Woolf's writing resists assimilation to any unified polemical position: it dramatizes contradictions, producing forms in which, as Pamela Transue notes, "every quality implies its opposite" (167). In fact, many readers, whatever their critical or political orientation, read Woolf's work as essentially contradictory: from a humanistic perspective, Alex Zwerdling writes that Woolf creates a "structure that allows rival codes to coexist rather than forcing the reader to choose between them" (207);[5] in *Feminine Fictions: Revisiting the Postmodern*, Patricia Waugh argues that "Woolf is clearly acutely aware of the extent to which

one's sense of self is a *theory* of the self constructed out of available
social practices and discourses. . . . Continuity is based, therefore,
upon one's ability to assimilate and relate dispersed and contradictory discourses to form a 'whole'" (95).

   In addition to the fiction itself, a range of autobiographical evidence demonstrates the extent of Woolf's ambivalence. Woolf's letters and diaries show that her feelings and attitudes are frequently
contradictory. She resented the intrusion and distraction of London
society and insisted that she despised parties, but she would always
return to London and rarely turned down a social invitation unless
she was ill. Of intellectuals, she wrote, "I've struggled and rebelled
against them all my life, but their integrity always makes me their
slave. Much though I hate Cambridge, and bitterly though I've suffered from it, I still respect it" (*Letters* 4:155). Reading an old article she had written, she said, "Good God, what a prig that woman
must be" (*Letters* 4:155), but elsewhere Woolf characterized herself as quite liberal. She was, after all, able to discuss "the most
intimate details of sexual life" (*Letters* 4:159). She asserted that
when she moved to Bloomsbury she was "rather adventurous, for
those days; that is we were sexually very free" but also that she was
"always sexually cowardly. . . . My terror of real life has always kept
me in a nunnery" (*Letters* 4:180). However, if indeed she was
"sexually cowardly," she was hardly a prude: "If Eddy chooses to
plunge his poker in an ant heap or a woman or the next young man
he meets in Bond St. its [*sic*] all the same to me" (*Letters* 4:226).
Moreover, despite the feminist content of her work, especially in
such essays as *A Room of One's Own* and *Three Guineas*, Woolf did
not choose to identify herself as a feminist. When she wrote of lis-
tening to two young men, she carefully disassociated herself from
feminists: "*If I were a feminist* [their egotism] would throw great
light on the history of the sexes—such complete self-absorption:
such entire belief that a woman has nothing to do but listen" (*Letters* 4:312; emphasis mine). However, while disowning the label,
Woolf expressed feminist ideas and was very much aware of wom-
en's subordinate social and cultural status.

   By focusing on Woolf's ambivalence, I don't mean to suggest that
she was in fact any more ambivalent than many writers. But feminist criticism has not yet addressed fully the fact of her ambivalence
or the forms it took. More specifically, I want to suggest that in her
fiction Woolf developed writing strategies that would make public

the kinds of ambivalences and internal contradictions she experienced and at the same time, as in the ambivalence of *To the Lighthouse* (1927), make it possible to conceal—to some extent—the political implications of these experiences. In short, she developed strategies that would allow her to break the "treaty of silence" and hide the fact—perhaps even from herself—that she was doing so. Toward this end, she combined oppositions: love could be inseparable from hate, identity from its absence. She sustained in her writing the most intense psychic conflicts and ambivalences, complexities that exist not only in representation but in the material conditions of women's lives and experiences.

The development of strategies that record ambivalence is related to Woolf's acute awareness of her own internalized boundaries, her sense of what she felt she—as a woman—could not or should not represent. These internalized boundaries, which enforce the "treaty of silence," are produced, Woolf argues, to a great extent by her experiences as a woman in the world. And when Woolf's work is read in the context of such twentieth-century women writers as Barnes and Duras, these boundaries seem particularly pronounced. In "Professions for Women," Woolf describes two "adventures" unique to her professional life that are inseparable from her gender. The first involves confronting and destroying her internalization of the "Angel in the House," the paradigm of Victorian womanhood, a voice within that urged her to review novels written by men uncritically, to be "sympathetic, be tender; flatter; deceive; use all the arts and wiles of our sex" (*Women and Writing* 59). Woolf points to the importance of her own privileged position when she writes that because she had an independent income and did not have to depend solely on charm for her living, she was able to turn on the Angel, grab her by the throat, and kill her. She describes this figurative act of violence as self-defense: "Had I not killed her she would have killed me" (59). In effect, she claims she successfully completes the difficult task of eliminating her own participation in one form of conventional female behavior. As many readers note, Lily Briscoe faces a similar task in coming to terms with Mrs. Ramsey in the most autobiographical of Woolf's novels, *To the Lighthouse*. It is only when Lily looks at the steps where she has previously imagined Mrs. Ramsey to be sitting (in "perfect goodness," "casting her shadow"), finds them empty, and is—at least for that moment—not overcome by nostalgia and loss that she can have her vision and finish her painting. The project of transforming oneself into an artist who represents instead of being represented by others is a difficult enterprise fraught with ambivalence—particularly for a woman. Lily must rid herself of Mrs. Ramsey's shadow; Woolf must rid herself of what she thinks a woman should be. But to lose Mrs. Ramsey and the comfort, security, and warmth of conventional representations of femininity is to suffer a great loss.

Woolf's second adventure involves her less successful struggle to write beyond socially approved subjects. With a major psychological obstacle removed and no material barriers in her way, what, Woolf asks, stands in the way of her just being herself in her writing? She doesn't know. She doesn't believe anyone else knows yet either. The reason, she believes, is that women have been historically unable to overcome powerful social constraints against their speaking freely and honestly of the body and its desires. And so they are silent—or indirect. The language Woolf uses to make her point is highly figurative and indirect, itself an indication of the point she is making, though she becomes more explicit at the end of the passage:

I want you to figure to yourselves a girl sitting with a pen in her hand, which for minutes, and indeed for hours, she never dips into the inkpot. The image that comes to my mind when I think of this girl is the image of a fisherman lying sunk in dreams on the verge of a deep lake with a rod held out over the water. She was letting her imagination sweep unchecked round every rock and cranny of the world that lies submerged in the depths of our unconscious being. Now came the experience, the experience that I believe to be far commoner with women writers than with men. The line raced through the girl's fingers. Her imagination had rushed away. It had sought the pools, the depths, the dark places where the largest fish slumber. And then there was a smash. There was an explosion. There was foam and confusion. The imagination had dashed itself against something hard. The girl was roused from her dream. She was indeed in a state of the most acute and difficult distress. To speak without figure she had thought of something, something about the body, about the passions which it was unfitting for her as a woman to say. Men, her reason told her, would be shocked. The consciousness of what men will say of a woman who speaks the truth about her passions had roused her from her artist's state of unconsciousness. She could write no more. The trance was over. Her imagination could work no longer. (*Women and Writing* 61–62)

To speak the absolute truth about the body as she experienced it was an obstacle Woolf felt unable to surmount. Even in this passage she depersonalizes passion by saying "the" body instead of "my" body and "body" instead of "female body," and she distances the image even further from herself by using the third person. But it does not follow from this that she was unaware of her body or its passions: her description demonstrates just the opposite. If she avoided writing explicitly about her body, sexuality, and the unconscious, it was not because of any personal problem unique to her. As Woolf points out, it is doubtful whether *any* woman had yet been able to write honestly about such matters. Her analysis suggests the reasons for women's silence about the body are structural rather than idiosyncratic. That is, they are embedded in institutions and social practices and then inscribed upon the individual subjects engaged in such practices. Her analysis also indicates that she connects her inability to write about the body with being male-defined.[6]

The move to Bloomsbury created conditions favorable to Woolf's efforts to push back boundaries of "acceptable" female behavior and expression. Much has been made of Bloomsbury as an elite, effete, educated enclave of privilege and decadence. If it was all these things it was more: for Woolf it was a place of expansion and growth, a place where she could risk breaking cultural taboos. There was little that could not be discussed: in "Old Bloomsbury," Woolf recalls Lytton Strachey pointing to a stain on Vanessa's white dress:

> "Semen?" he said.
> Can one really say it? I thought and we burst out laughing. With that one word all barriers of reticence and reserve went down. A flood of the sacred fluid seemed to overwhelm us. Sex permeated our conversation. The word bugger was never far from our lips. We discussed copulation with the same excitement and openness that we had discussed the nature of good. It is strange to think how reticent, how reserved we had been and for how long. (*Moments of Being* 195–196)

Taboos could be broken here, and discussing sex and sexuality in mixed company was just one example. Woolf's language, especially the image of being overwhelmed by a flood of semen, is certainly at odds with traditional images of her as reticent, withdrawn, and Victorian.

Moreover, it was to the Bloomsbury group that Woolf described George Duckworth's unwanted sexual attentions, breaking the "treaty of silence" whereby incest victims often try to protect their abusers. Recent work on incest demonstrates that victims often have complicated and conflicting responses to caretakers who abuse them, including the desire to protect the abuser, which makes it difficult to speak out publicly to expose what is happening. Although George Duckworth was Woolf's half brother, not her parent, after Woolf's mother died George filled in part a parental, caretaker role. He was, after all, sixteen years older than Woolf. In "22 Hyde Park Gate" Woolf writes that he was both caretaker and abuser: "Yes, the old ladies of Kensington and Belgravia never knew that George Duckworth was not only father and mother, brother and sister to those poor Stephen girls; he was their lover also" (*Moments of Being* 177). It is hard to discern from this statement the extent of George's abuse, in part because Woolf wrote "22 Hyde Park Gate" to entertain the Bloomsbury Memoir Club and also because she gives the statement a certain playful, rhetorical flourish by using it dramatically to conclude her memoir. But Woolf did tell people of George's behavior, both directly and indirectly, as Louise DeSalvo documents in *Virginia Woolf: The Impact of Childhood Sexual Abuse on Her Life and Work.*[7]

If the extent of George's abuse is unclear, it is clear that from Woolf's perspective George transgressed boundaries she wanted him to respect, leaving her with feelings of shame and resentment. Read in the context of Woolf's description of George's behavior in *Moments of Being*, other comments, such as the diary entry of May 25, 1926, are suggestive: "The heat has come, bringing with it the inexplicably disagreeable memories of parties, & George Duckworth; a fear haunts me even now, as I drive past Park Lane on top of a bus" (*Diaries* 3:87). And George was not the only half brother to transgress acceptable boundaries. But the first direct indication of her other half brother Gerald's abuse, which occurred when she was only six or seven, is in "A Sketch of the Past," written in 1939 toward the end of her life.[8] DeSalvo points out that "embedded in

Virginia's retelling of her memory is the idea that *she herself* was responsible for causing what happened to her: she says she remembered 'resenting, disliking it'; but she also says that she believed 'it is wrong to allow' parts of the body 'to be touched.' . . . she had already been taught that if something bad happens to you if you are a girl, it is your own fault; indeed, Victorian ideology held girls responsible for the morality of their brothers" (108). Woolf's belief that she was somehow complicit in what had happened to her caused her to remain silent about or repress these episodes—at least in her writing—until late in her life.

In contrast to her internalized restraints, the material obstacles Woolf faced in writing what and as she wished were uncommonly few. With Leonard Woolf, she founded her own press. That her unparalleled economic and intellectual freedom still did not release her from internalized constraints and conflicts contradicts her own position that under the correct conditions art could be free from social, political, and other ideological influences, though it is certainly also true that these very influences shape one's subjective experience of one's freedom (or lack thereof). Material forces do inscribe subjectivity: total freedom from such forces is a fantasy. But with the important qualification that subjectivity is always so inscribed, Woolf's assessment of her position is true enough: "I'm the only woman in England free to write what I like. The others must be thinking of series & editors" (*Diaries* 3:43). (Only with *The Voyage Out* [1915] and *Night and Day* [1919], which were published by George Duckworth, did Woolf have to think about editors' criticisms of her fiction.) Woolf's experience publishing her own fiction could hardly be more different from that of most authors, including Djuna Barnes who had a difficult and frustrating time getting *Nightwood* accepted for publication and then, once it was accepted, had to submit it to considerable editorial revision. Woolf writes: "When the publishers told me to write what they liked I said No, I'll publish myself and write what I like" (*Letters* 4:348). To a great extent true, this assertion of freedom doesn't speak to all the subtle complexities of her experiences, since there were other obstacles Woolf wished to surmount but could not, obstacles she, like Lily Briscoe in *To the Lighthouse*, found masculine, authoritative, and terrible because violent. Yet she could not rid herself of these obstacles by recognizing and naming them.

At the same time that it enabled her to shape contradictory ex-

periences and ambivalent attitudes, Woolf's fiction provided ways
for her to begin to represent what many writers of her time and
class could not articulate explicitly in their work, the taboo subjects
of the unconscious, desire, and sexuality. As Woolf recognized, "you
must allow for the fact that many kinds of writing are forbidden the
professional writer—a sad fact, but a fact" (*Letters* 4:234). In what
follows, I examine not only the strategies Woolf developed both as a
writer and as a woman to attempt to break the treaty of silence in
ways acceptable to her but also how these strategies, by obscuring
the radical critiques being made, reduced the risks inherent in
breaking this treaty. I discuss three texts, *To the Lighthouse, The
Waves*, and *Between the Acts*, because together they demonstrate
some of the different forms ambivalence takes in Woolf's fiction.[9]
To the Lighthouse, as the most autobiographical of her fiction, illu-
minates Woolf's own dilemma as a woman writer in a male-dominated society. In her representation of the way Lily Briscoe is able
to finish her painting, Woolf suggests some of the reasons why lyrical prose was such a powerful tool in her own writing. Rhythm and
repetition, not adherence to Mr. Ramsey's kind of philosophical linear coherence, enable Lily to finish her painting and for a moment
allow her to get beyond both internal and external barriers to her
work. But it is in *The Waves* that Woolf explores most fully in practice what it means to write to a rhythm and not to a plot. In the
context of her representation of Lily's use of rhythm in *To the Lighthouse*, Woolf's own lyrical method in *The Waves* is especially significant; she was attempting to chart new and distinctly female expressions of subjectivity and the world. *The Waves* is at once the most
lyrical and experimental of the novels and the least political, though
it is true that while Woolf tried to keep art and politics separate she
was ultimately unable to do so. In *Between the Acts*, Woolf recognizes and rejects the ambivalence produced by her subjective lyrical experiments and her internalization of the treaty of silence. *Between the Acts* represents most explicitly the extent of women's vulnerability in the world, though paradoxically, it accomplishes this
through methods more indirect than direct.

Masculinity is inscribed as an external obstacle to women's freedom, autonomy, and creativity in *To the Lighthouse*, for if the moment of Lily's creation is free from the pressure of Mrs. Ramsey,
it is less certain how free it is from the pressure of Mr. Ramsey.
Moments before completing the picture Lily is able to give Mr.

Ramsey—in his absence—"whatever she had wanted to give him, when he left her that morning" (308–309). Is it the sympathy Mr. Ramsey had demanded and Lily felt herself unable to provide? Woolf leaves room for doubt with the vagueness of "whatever." It could be sympathy, but it could also be something else perhaps based not so much on Mr. Ramsey's definition of what he wants from her as on her own formulation of what she is willing or able to give—or perhaps it ceases to matter what it is exactly when Lily is distracted by her painting. The moment at which she is able to give this "whatever" to him, a moment which is from Lily's perspective one of tolerance and compassion, is crowned by her mystical connection with another man, Mr. Carmichael. Carmichael, who is also an artist, has submitted neither to Mrs. Ramsey's feminine charms nor to Mr. Ramsey's masculine ideas of order. (Carmichael alone causes Mrs. Ramsey to doubt herself; moreover, he will have his second bowl of soup if he wants it, regardless of Mr. Ramsey's rage.) Thus, this mystical moment of connection with Carmichael is significant: it is a way to empower Lily, but it is also a retreat on Woolf's part from imagining a resolution to the obstacle Mr. Ramsey poses to Lily's art.

Mr. Ramsey remains an obstacle and becomes a part of Lily's art, inseparable from it, contributing to the sense that rival codes coexist. Lily completes the painting but does not rid herself of Mr. Ramsey as she rids herself of Mrs. Ramsey. Like the lighthouse, where Mr. Ramsey has landed, her canvas appears blurred, which links him with her picture. When she completes the final stroke it is an uncertain gesture: like an act of faith, it is only by pressing on "*as if* she saw it clear for a second" (310, emphasis mine) that she can finish. The formidable boundary Mr. Ramsey symbolizes for Lily is not successfully negotiated or resolved, even if she momentarily makes a sort of peace with him. It is a boundary that is at once blurred and emphatically articulated by the line she draws down the center of her canvas (and mirrored by the line Woolf drew down the center of the last page of her manuscript). And it is a peace she must make in order to work.

Lily's anger at Mr. Ramsey's demands, however justified, impedes her art. To work, she thinks she must "achieve that razor edge of balance between two opposite forces; Mr. Ramsey and the picture; which was necessary" (287). While this image of the "razor edge of balance" suggests that the tension itself is necessary, given the force that Mr. Ramsey represents Lily doesn't have much choice. If she is to work she must work within her experience of him as a constraint. It becomes inseparable from her art, for Lily's vision articulates the boundary Mr. Ramsey symbolizes: paradoxically, the act of completing the painting reproduces the boundary that she must be able to cross—but cannot—in order to create freely, without obstacle.

If writing ambivalence was a way for Woolf to move closer to the boundaries she could never successfully move beyond—the prohibition against writing the body or desire, the fear of what men would think of her—it was a conscious and strategic choice for writing at the edge of the socially permissible. It was not the discovery of an inherently feminine or subversive form; it was the development of a form that, within the contexts in which it was used and in relation to the subjects it explores, enabled Woolf—and other women writers, including Barnes and Duras—to be at once within and without ideology. It was not, therefore, a form naturally expressive of the female body as it might exist in nature, outside culture. That Lily Briscoe experiences similar inhibitions and attempts to resolve them in similar ways shows the extent to which Woolf was conscious of how language's rhythmic properties could be used to overturn rhetorical structures and internalized constraints. But she does not claim this writing is inherently feminine: when Woolf writes of a "woman's sentence" as in the following oft-quoted passage from "Dorothy Richardson," she is not describing a sentence that could only have been written by a woman:

> She has invented, or, if she has not invented, developed and applied to her own uses, a sentence which we might call the psychological sentence of the feminine gender. It is of a more elastic fibre than the old, capable of stretching to the extreme, of suspending the frailest particles, of enveloping the vaguest shapes. Other writers of the opposite sex have used sentences of this description and stretched them to the extreme. But there is a difference. Miss Richardson has fashioned her sentence consciously, in order that it may descend to the depths and investigate the crannies of Miriam Henderson's consciousness. It is a woman's sentence, but only in the sense that it is used to describe a woman's mind by a writer who is neither proud nor afraid of anything that she may discover in the psychology of her sex. (*Women and Writing* 191)

What Woolf means by the "psychological sentence of the female gender" or a "woman's sentence" is linked not to some unmediated experience of the body but rather to a strategic *use.* The sentence is shaped through conscious and creative effort; it does not flow as naturally from the body as menstrual fluid or urine in the way that we are invited in the last chapter of Joyce's *Ulysses* to see Molly Bloom's words flowing from her body without conscious shaping and control.

Nevertheless, there are reasons why writing that emphasizes its own rhythms and diffuseness is well suited to Woolf's project of representing something of female subjectivity and desire. It produces a vagueness about boundaries, a feature of Woolf's novels and perhaps a feature of a female relationship to the world and otherness. As James Naremore notes, "personality itself becomes dissolved in total communion with what is 'out there'" (36). The experience of dissolving the self is common in Woolf's novels. Lily Briscoe describes her desire for unity with Mrs. Ramsey in language that is at once erotic and mystical:

> What art was there, known to love or cunning, by which one pressed through into those secret chambers? What device for becoming, like waters poured into one jar, inextricably the same, one with the object one adored? Could the body achieve, or the mind, subtly mingling in the intricate passages of the brain? or the heart? Could loving, as people called it, make her and Mrs. Ramsey one? for it was not knowledge but unity she desired, not inscriptions on tablets, nothing that could be written in any language known to men, but intimacy itself, which is knowledge. (79)

And yet, Lily proclaims, "Nothing happened. Nothing! Nothing!" (79), as she leaned her head against Mrs. Ramsey's knee. If Lily does have such an experience it is at the end of the text, in the mystical moment of compassion, understanding, and connection with Carmichael that mitigates her anger toward Mr. Ramsey and provides a way to connect with him too. In contrast to Lily, Mrs. Ramsey does have the experience of entering into otherness, of becoming the thing she looks at: "It was odd, she thought, how if one was alone, one leant to inanimate things; trees, streams, flowers; felt they expressed one; felt they became one; felt they knew one, in a sense were one" (97). While Clarissa Dalloway experiences

herself as part of people she never met, in *The Waves* Bernard remarks that "this is not one life; nor do I always know if I am man or
woman, Bernard or Neville, Louis, Susan, Jinny, or Rhoda—so
strange is the contact of one with another" (281). And in *Between
the Acts*, Lucy Swithin comments wistfully, "We live in others. . . .
We live in things" (70).

Naremore states that such impulses signal the "uneasy compromises the characters make between the will to live in the world and
the temptation to dissolve all individuality and sink into a deathlike
trance" (55). But if the dissolution of boundaries between the per-
ceiver and the external world produces ambivalence and uneasy
compromises, the choices they negotiate are perhaps not as stark as
Naremore suggests. As Rachel Blau DuPlessis has argued, the dissolution of individuality is not just death: "The communal protago-
nist is a way of organizing the work so that neither the development
of an individual against a backdrop of supporting characters nor the
formation of a heterosexual couple is central to the novel" (163).
The diffusion of the boundary between self and other becomes a
way for Woolf to break the structuring devices of the marriage plot
or the traditional quest plot and to explore new stories, possibilities,
and knowledge. Lily's language in particular indicates that she
longs for an intimacy that is knowledge—but a new form of knowing, "nothing that could be written in any language known to men"
(79). The refusal to maintain a clear boundary between oneself and
the world is a radical view of the relationship between self and other
where the mingling of self and other is not just death and
annihilation of the self but a restorative wholeness and life-affirm-
ing intimacy. It is rather the lack of connection maintained by distinct boundaries that pervades Woolf's writing as absence and loss.

Nancy Chodorow's work on the social production of gender and
sexuality in the context of the mother-daughter relationship reveals
profound differences between women's and men's experiences of
self and other within existing social structures.[10] Both sexes face
the same task in separating from the mother (the primary caretaker
in most families) given the intense ambivalence of such a close connection. For girls, however, gender identification with the mother
makes total separation impossible. The perception of similarity and
sameness runs counter to the need for difference. For boys, of
course, sexual difference is visible and tangible, apparent not only
to themselves but to their mothers, who, Chodorow argues, "tend to

create boundaries in relation to sons and to treat them as a differ-
entiated other" ("Mothering" 146). This difference enables the boy
to separate himself from his mother's omnipotence and gain a sense
of otherness. His sexual difference symbolizes his masculinity and
separateness, both of which are desirable within and reinforced by
larger cultural contexts. But a girl does not have something different and desirable with which to oppose her mother. Equally important, Chodorow points out, the mother does not cathect her daughter in the same way as she does her son: whereas the son is a sexual
other, the daughter becomes part of a narcissistically defined self.
No child has any control of the mother's differentiation between son
and daughter in relation to herself. Perhaps because of this extended, unresolved relationship with their mothers, more women
than men experience a confusion of boundaries and connection
with others and the world. But because so much psychoanalytic
theory is male-centered, what gets talked about are the *disadvan-
tages* of this early developmental situation for the daughter. To see
the diffusion of boundaries and self as a disadvantage is to subscribe
to a certain ideology about the world and the primacy of the autono-
mous individual over community that Woolf herself rejects. Still,
even if a girl's early identification with her mother results in an
orientation to otherness profoundly different from a boy's, that experience is but one of many such experiences that must occur in
order to structure and compose subjects who relate to the world in
different ways depending on their gender.

   To the Lighthouse destabilizes gender-specific ways of being in
the world as part of a larger project of portraying psychic conflicts
rooted in gender, including women's reticence to voice their experiences in a radically unsettling or subversive manner. In the
first section, Woolf's use of naturalizing imagery often produces a
sense of behavior rooted in the biology of sexual difference. When
Mr. Ramsey intrudes on Mrs. Ramsey and their son James, Woolf
describes his demands for sympathy in language suggesting a heterosexual intercourse and economy that depend upon a distinct di-
chotomy between the sexes. Mrs. Ramsey is female fertility. Because her body gives birth, her power comes from her natural ability
to "surround and protect [until there is] scarcely a shell of herself
left for her to know herself by" (60). Her reproductive capacity is
translated into social significance not only for her husband and children but for herself. Characterized as male sterility, "barren and

bare," Mr. Ramsey and his demands suggest phallic violence: he
plunges and smotes like a "beak of brass" (58).

Their social intercourse inscribes itself as the equivalent of sexual
intercourse in James's consciousness. What begins as omniscient
narration becomes inseparable from James's perception of what is
occurring between his parents and his own attempt to supplement
his mother's lack of male power:

> standing between her knees, very stiff, James felt all her
> strength flaring up to be drunk and quenched by the beak of
> brass, the arid scimitar of the male, which smote mercilessly,
> again and again, demanding sympathy. . . .
>
> James, as he stood stiff between her knees, felt her rise in a
> rosy-flowered fruit tree laid with leaves and dancing boughs into
> which the beak of brass, the arid scimitar of his father, the ego-
> tistical man, plunged and smote, demanding sympathy. (59–60)

Woolf emphasizes James's hostility toward his father and his own
identification with masculinity. It is as if James, standing stiff, tries
to make himself into the phallus his mother lacks. The images attached to James and his father are hard and unbending in contrast
to Mrs. Ramsey, a difference that is later reinscribed in James's and
Cam's varying responses to their father on the voyage to the lighthouse and in James's position as lawmaker in relation to Cam.

Dichotomized sexual difference, however, is produced by James's
own internal economy and language as a result of what he observes
and intuits. That is, its origins are social rather than inherent or
natural. His mother's response causes him to imagine her as a flow-
ering tree, and Mr. Ramsey's single-minded, incessant need produces the image of a beak of brass. External images of objects in-
teract with, even produce internal reality and subjectivity: "The
wheelbarrow, the lawnmower, the sound of poplar trees, leaves
whitening before rain, rooks cawing, brooms knocking, dresses rus-
tling—all these were so coloured and distinguished in [James's]
mind that he already had his private code, his secret language,
though he appeared the image of stark and uncompromising sev-
erity" (10). While his uncompromising look makes his mother distinguish him from herself (as she will not distinguish other women,
regardless of their demeanor) and imagine him in masculine terms—
as a participant in the world of men, as a judge or important public
official—James' sensuous interior language aligns him more with

his mother and Lily than with Mr. Ramsey (or the figure upon whom his worst characteristics are projected, Charles Tansley). For like Lily, he thinks in images, whereas Mr. Ramsey's mind works linearly. When Mr. Ramsey reaches Q he tries to push himself on to the next logical step, which is R: "Q he was sure of. Q he could demonstrate. If Q then is Q—R—. . . 'Then R . . .' He braced himself. He clenched himself" (54). By thinking in images, or in the language of literature rather than philosophy, James complicates the dichotomized sexual difference produced in these passages. In the process of producing images he partakes in what, according to the economy of sexual difference, is feminine not masculine.[11]

The sexual polarities in Woolf's writing are sometimes compared to those in D. H. Lawrence's work, where dichotomized sexual difference is essential to a generative, mystical contact of sexual opposites. This contact is the only entrance to a sexual/spiritual reality that is ahistorical and transcendent—a reality that is, for instance, open to each generation in *The Rainbow* despite the different historical circumstances forced upon each by social and industrial changes. Impersonal and essentialist in that it depends upon each partner being what he or she *is* (male or female) apart from history and being open to the sexual mystery and challenge of the other, the contact is potentially renewing or depleting for each partner. Each may gain temporary ascendance—but the process is dialectical and progress more ambiguously circular than linear. For Lawrence, the goal is an equilibrium reached through sexual difference: the pleasures and prices are different but equivalent for each sex. When either seeks more vulgar types of power over the other the result is destructive, as in the relationship between Gudrun and Gerald in *Women in Love*.

Woolf, in contrast to Lawrence, unravels the economy of sexual difference and uses sexual polarities to suggest that the pleasures and prices of heterosexual exchange are not equal. After the encounter with his wife Mr. Ramsey is "restored, renewed," so filled with "humble gratitude" that he will do her the favor of taking a turn watching the children (60). While it is true that she experiences "the rapture of successful creation," she is exhausted and depleted from the effort, which is essentially an effort to renew her husband, not herself. Although dissatisfied afterward, she not only doesn't know why she feels this way, she doesn't want to know why. She tries to keep herself from putting "into words her dissatisfaction," preferring to let the reasons remain unarticulated and unknown (60). Despite her efforts, she realizes that she is unwilling to admit her strength or the extent of her self-assertion: she is unwilling, even for a moment, to "feel finer" than her husband. And yet, in spite of herself, in this exchange she does feel superior and strong. It's hard to see how she could feel otherwise, though, since she is required to assert a power more maternal than sexual. Their exchange turns her husband into a son; he becomes "like a child who drops off satisfied" (60), which reverses her more comfortable experience of herself as inferior to her husband.

The essential features of this exchange between the Ramseys are repeated in the exchange between Mr. Ramsey and Lily in the final section and work at cross purposes with the resolutions Woolf attempts. As he did in the past with his wife, Mr. Ramsey comes to Lily for sympathy. Initially, she refuses him, articulating a more general refusal of the traditional heterosexual system. But her refusal is ambivalent, her desires contradictory, for she subsequently realizes that *she* wants Mr. Ramsey: "And as if she had something she must share, yet could hardly leave her easel, so full her mind was of what she was thinking, of what she was seeing, Lily went past Mr. Carmichael holding her brush to the edge of the lawn. Where was the boat now? And Mr. Ramsey? She wanted him" (300).

Although there is a shift here—Lily is not Mrs. Ramsey, not the Angel of the House, she keeps her painting in mind and brush in hand—the structure and effects in the present are much the same as those of the past. When Mr. Ramsey lands at the lighthouse he is youthful and renewed. He literally springs from the boat, "lightly like a young man" (308). At the moment when Lily realizes he "must have reached it," she suddenly feels "completely tired out [from] the effort of looking at [the lighthouse] and the effort of thinking of him landing there" (308). And yet these final pages also suggest the possibility of change, of breaking out of established, comfortable, or oppressive patterns. Moments before landing, when Cam and James dread their father's predictable response (the lines he has been quoting all day, beginning with "But I beneath a rougher sea" and including "We perished, each alone"), he breaks the pattern which has produced their expectations: "If he did, they could not bear it; they would shriek aloud; they could not endure another explosion of the passion that boiled in him; but to their surprise all he said was 'Ah' as if he thought to himself, But why make a fuss about that?" (305–306). Because the dynamic between them is at least temporarily altered and fixed in a significant moment, they too become freer to respond to him in different ways. There is, however, no reason to believe that this resolution, even though it is weighted rhetorically by occurring at the end of the text, is the last word on Mr. Ramsey's relationship with his children. Given the fluidity of any particular feeling in the text, it is much easier to believe that this moment, like the others, is fleeting.

The patterns Lily breaks in this last section are striking and, as many critics have noted, parallel Woolf's own creative process in working with autobiographical material. As Lily comes to terms with her surrogate mother, Mrs. Ramsey, so too Woolf claimed to come to terms with her own dead mother, Julia Stephen. (The finality of this resolution, however, given the complexities and intense ambivalence of the mother-daughter relationship, seems suspect.) In addition to Lily's conscious recognition of her debt to Mrs. Ramsey and her insight into Mrs. Ramsey's creativity in the domestic realm, Woolf establishes further connections between them. Both Lily and Mrs. Ramsey experience language as a force that alienates and entraps. As Mrs. Ramsey responds to the steady rhythm of the strokes of light from the lighthouse, she becomes the light, which lifts up on itself "some little phrase or other which had been lying in her mind" (97). In this instance, what begins with words she chooses leads unexpectedly to words she rejects:

> "Children don't forget, children don't forget"—which she would repeat and begin adding to it, It will end, it will end, she said. It will come, it will come, when suddenly she added, We are in the hands of the Lord.
>
> But instantly she was annoyed with herself for saying that. Who had said it? Not she; she had been trapped into saying something she did not mean. (97)

Although Mrs. Ramsey does not believe any lord could have made such an unjust world, the ritualistic language comes to mind by virtue of its rhythm, not its significance. Similarly, Lily is haunted by words which she does not believe or choose to think but which, inscribed in her mind, she cannot rid herself of. For Lily it is Charles Tansley's incantation, "women can't write, women can't paint," that comes unbidden: "She heard some voice saying she couldn't paint, she couldn't create, as if she were caught up in one of those habitual currents in which after a certain time experience forms in the mind, so that one repeats words without being aware any longer who originally spoke them" (237). In order to escape the traps of language, the ways men's words have been inscribed in her mind, Lily turns to her body—not because as a woman she is more aligned with it, but because her experience of it is as an unmapped and unarticulated field.

Lily wants to portray "one's body feeling, not one's mind" (265). Charles's words echo in her mind, ironically losing their significance and hold by their very repetition, producing instead a rhythm that fuels Lily's creative energies. Woolf describes this process in somatic images:

> For the mass loomed before her; it protruded; she felt it pressing on her eyeballs. Then, as if some juice necessary for the lubrication of her faculties were spontaneously squirted, she began precariously dipping among the blues and umbers, moving her brush hither and thither . . . as if it had fallen in with some rhythm which was dictated to her . . . by what she saw, so that while her hand quivered with life, this rhythm was strong enough to bear her along with it on its current. Certainly she was losing consciousness of outer things. And as she lost consciousness of outer things, and her name and her personality and her appearance . . . her mind kept throwing up from its depths, scenes, and names, and memories and ideas, like a fountain spurting over that glaring, hideously difficult white space. (237–238)

Ironically, Lily uses the rhythm of words that insist upon her own artistic incompetence ("women can't write, women can't paint") as a vehicle for creative expression. The rhythm of the words becomes the rhythm of what she sees, producing what she sees. The way Woolf combines physical and mental processes in the passage suggests a close relationship between not just the body and visual images (Lily's medium) but the body and language (Woolf's medium).

Julia Kristeva's theory of poetic language offers a useful perspective from which to view Woolf's lyrical writing.[12] For Kristeva, all language records a dialectical process between symbolic and semiotic properties. The symbolic is the realm of repression, signification, structure, and law. It produces meaning; it is logical and linear. The semiotic is linked to pre-Oedipal bodily drives and energies. Its pulses and rhythms constantly threaten the stability of linear meaning, even in "ordinary" prose. Because Kristeva's semiotic continues to disturb the symbolic, it is misleading to think that the dialectic between it and the symbolic is resolved at any particular moment. Nor is the semiotic entirely without structure, since it is conditioned by the body's regulating processes: it is not, therefore, the conceptual opposite of the symbolic, and impulses to link the two in a dichotomous structure should be resisted. To do so would be to reinstitute a structure that Kristeva rejects. Although what she means by poetic language is a structuring and destructuring practice, Kristeva also distinguishes her work from deconstructive practices that dismantle traditional structures and mastery in order to gather all power to the deconstructor.[13]

With Lily Briscoe's lyrical experience, Woolf depicts a woman's attempt to produce an alternative representation of female experience, and she shows just how difficult such an enterprise can be when so many internal and external factors conspire to prevent it. Lily is distracted by Mr. Ramsey and by her own internalized system of restraint. In order to escape convention and to move beyond cultural inscriptions, Lily—and Woolf herself—switches from a dependence on what Kristeva calls the symbolic to an exploration of the possibilities inherent in the semiotic. What Kristeva calls the semiotic enabled Woolf to negotiate the risks of representing female experience of the world, of making the unknown known. It became a way for Woolf to represent her experience of her body and her desires from a very different perspective than that of the dominant male culture. It is this attempt to shape previously unrepresented territories of a woman's experience of the world, her own body, and her desires—what she tells us her lyricism means in *To the Lighthouse*—that separates Woolf from male writers whose literary style is equally "poetic."[14]

Of all Woolf's fiction, *The Waves* foregrounds these semiotic impulses most emphatically. It also demonstrates most fully how rhythm can embody a subversive desire for liberation from confining social and political structures. Woolf's most radical literary experiment, *The Waves* is also the least obviously political in content, although its form subverts traditional narrative and the ideologies it supports. Woolf was very much aware that her use of rhythm in *The Waves* disrupts traditional literary forms: "I am writing to a rhythm and not to a plot. . . . though the rhythmical is more natural to me than narrative, it is completely opposed to the tradition of fiction"

(*Letters* 4:204). Like Lily Briscoe and Mrs. Ramsey, Woolf uses rhythm in a way that is antithetical to tradition, meaning, and logical sequence.[15] She doesn't abandon sequence entirely, since the text does proceed chronologically. Nor does she forego meaning, since to do so would either be to become like Rhoda—entirely disconnected from the world—or, as Kristeva suggests, to pretend to give up all power only to retain it and therefore become the only person capable of truly deciphering the strange new code. But rhythm and repetition disrupt and fragment sequence and plot, producing a text with lapses of consciousness similar to the dissolutions the figures themselves experience. And this rhythm is more "natural" to her, Woolf claims, than narrative.

Despite discrete events such as the dinner parties and Rhoda's suicide, Woolf does not subject the six lives she portrays to the structuring demands of narrative. Instead, everything is subordinated to rhythm. No single voice is privileged over the others; in fact, traces of individuality or idiosyncrasy in tone are effaced by the rhythm. The voices all sound the same, and each remains the same from childhood to old age, even though they describe different experiences and perceptions. We move from consciousness to consciousness as the voices separate from and then merge with one another, an experience the speakers themselves share. As Bernard says, "We melt into each other with phrases. We are edged with mist. We make an unsubstantial territory" (16).

Because in *The Waves* formal and ideological subversion simultaneously retreat from political content, Woolf's experiment with language resists oppressive conventions only in part and with a great deal of ambivalence. Rather than making its "meaning" clear, the text diffuses meaning with language that emphasizes its own rhythmic properties—making meaning as fleeting as the image of the fin that rises up out of "the wastes of silence" (273)—and situates itself in the unsettling territory between sense and nonsense. The fin is sharply defined, precise: the sea surrounding it is diffuse and engulfing. But as in the text where moments of clarity emerge out of rhythmic and diffuse expanses of prose, the fin rises out of the vast expanse of the sea. The speakers experience subjectivity in a similar way: at times they feel their identities are discrete; at times the boundaries between them and others blur, creating an undifferentiated whole.

When Bernard's identity dissipates, rhythm produces a flow of words that results in very little meaning. As with Mrs. Ramsey and Lily Briscoe in *To the Lighthouse*, rhythm and repetition, because unstructured and yet patterned according to a different "logic," challenge the notion of an individual in control of his or her thoughts:

> So into the street again, swinging my stick, looking at wire trays in stationers' shop-windows, at baskets of fruit grown in the colonies, murmuring Pillicock sat on Pillicock's hill, or Hark, hark, the dogs do bark, or The world's great age begins anew, or Come away, come away, death—mingling nonsense and poetry, floating in the stream. Something always has to be done next. Tuesday follows Monday; Wednesday, Tuesday. Each spreads the same ripple. The being grows rings, like a tree. Like a tree, leaves fall. (282–283)

Formally innovative and subversive in the ways it destabilizes and decenters the individual human subject, *The Waves* produces an aesthetic strangely at odds with the subversiveness of its form, an aesthetic intoxicated by the possibilities of language itself. Woolf characterized herself as "led on irresistibly by the lure of some phrase" (*Letters* 4:203), and nowhere is this more apparent than in *The Waves*. What results is prose that obfuscates its political critique.

The Waves does make a political critique. Bernard moves from sense to nonsense at the precise moment the text opens up the space for a critique of Western imperialism. Looking at baskets of fruit from the colonies, Bernard thinks not of empire and its political implications. His language and its rhythms lead instead to childish nonsense: "Pillicock sat on Pillicock's hill." But Pillicock is an imperialistic figure of British control: the image of sitting on his hill suggests ownership, control, and possession, while the name Pillicock inscribes a phallocentric presence. By following the lure of language in rhythmic, associative ways, Woolf shows how Bernard's subjectivity is contradictory at unconscious levels. He doesn't recognize what his words imply, yet these words have structured his consciousness. Rather than decisively pursuing the ideas these words make possible, Bernard drifts toward the sense of consolation rhythmic language can produce, as in the following repetitions: "Nevertheless, life is pleasant, life is tolerable. Tuesday follows Monday; then comes Wednesday. The mind grows rings; the iden-

tity becomes robust; pain is absorbed in growth" (257). Despite everything, life is "pleasant" and "tolerable." Life goes on, one might
as well say—or some such platitude. The loose repetition of the
passage shows how the text develops according to a "curve of
rhythm" rather than by a linear formula. Just a few pages later Bernard again reminds himself: "Life is pleasant. Life is good. . . .
Something always has to be done next. Tuesday follows Monday;
Wednesday Tuesday. Each spreads the same ripple of well-being,
repeats the same curve of rhythm; covers fresh sand with a chill or
ebbs a little slackly without. So the being grows rings; identity
becomes robust" (261–262). Bernard's resignation and mindless
repetition encourage passivity, acceptance, and drift rather than intellectual, active engagement aimed at identifying and challenging
the social conditions that lead to despair or boredom. Or, to put it
another way, the reader's experience merges with Bernard's to the
extent that the rhythm lulls him or her into complacency.

This sense of complacency is at odds with the text's representations of inequality and injustice, pain not ahistorical and universal
but local and tied to concrete situations. If Woolf chooses not to
pursue, critique, or discursively analyze these kinds of issues in
The Waves, she nevertheless includes them in significant ways.
That is to say, she inscribes contradiction, conflict, and ambivalence. Against the diffuse, rhythmic expanse of language as engulfing as the sea, discrete experiences of pain and oppression emerge
in sharp focus, much like the fin that rises in the ocean. Louis, for
example, suffers enormously from his sense of the inferiority of his
origins and thus of himself: "My father is a banker in Brisbane and
I speak with an Australian accent" (19). Even as an adult he looks
at the "little men at the next table to be sure that I do what they do"
(93). His class origins provide compelling reasons for why he suffers, even if he cares more than his friends do about his "inferior"
origins. He has internalized values that really do exist in his society
but which the text diffuses: whether or not his friends accept him,
Louis's pain remains, suggesting that attempts at local levels to alleviate suffering originating in social structures are at best partially
successful.

Like Louis, Rhoda is an outsider, hovering at the edge of society.
As a female, however, her position is even more tenuous, for no
work grounds her to the world. Being with others is a painful experience for her: with others around she loses her fragile connec-

tion to the world. Only in solitude does she feel safe, in that "short space of freedom" between encounters with others where her life is imaginative and rich: "I have picked all the fallen petals and made them swim. I have put raindrops in some. I will plant a lighthouse here, a head of sweet Alice. And I will now rock the brown basin from side to side so that my ships may ride the waves. Some will founder. Some will dash themselves against the cliffs. One sails alone. That is my ship. It sails into icy caverns where the sea-bear barks and stalactites swing green chains" (19). For Rhoda, the world is a frightening place, where "sea-bears bark and stalactites swing green chains." Her language is filled with vivid, active imagery: her imagination empowers her and makes her even more vulnerable. In her private space, she is able to create, but what she creates threatens her perception of her own balance and stability. She makes the petals into fragile boats. She causes the storm that threatens them by rocking the basin.

Ironically, Rhoda's encounter with culture and language—with things we usually think of as empowering—initiates her disintegration. School, a place where this encounter with the world occurs, shatters her sense of herself as a person capable of action. She experiences herself instead as powerless and incapable and therefore as radically different from the others:

> The others look; they look with understanding. Louis writes; Susan writes; even Bernard has now begun to write. But I cannot write. I see only figures. The others are handing in their answers, one by one. Now it is my turn. But I have no answer. The others are allowed to go. They slam the door. Miss Hudson goes. I am left alone to find an answer. The figures mean nothing now. Meaning has gone. The clock ticks. The two hands are convoys marching through a desert. The black bars on the clock face are green oases. The long hand has marched ahead to find water. The other painfully stumbles among hot stones in the desert. It will die in the desert. (21)

Rhoda's imagination makes the clock into something wonderfully creative, but she represents herself as passive and powerless. As her imagination takes hold and the clock takes on a whole new life, she is no longer the subject of the sentence capable of effecting change or initiating action. When she is the subject she asserts her inability to do anything ("I cannot write. . . . I have no answer"). Rhoda is the text's most vulnerable figure though the source of her vulnerability remains vague, mysterious, and unarticulated. If Louis's class background offers an explanation for his sense of inferiority, no explicit cause is offered to account for Rhoda's acute fear of the world and of other people. As Bernard wonders, "What fear wavered and hid itself and blew to a flame in the depths of her grey, her startled, her dreaming eyes? Cruel and vindictive as we are, we are not bad to that extent" (252). Like Barnes's Robin Vote and Duras's Lol V. Stein, Woolf's Rhoda is radically separated from others by her different relationship to language (or lack of such a relationship) and by her distance from culture. This radical separation becomes for Barnes a way to figure what society represses and for Duras a way to both explore unconscious drives and desires and subvert discourses of mastery and control. For Woolf, however, it is a way to express how frightening disintegration of personality can be and how it renders one incapable of taking up a meaningful position in either discourse or the material world.

Rhoda's exclusion from language suggests the restricted ways women can participate in culture. She has no place. Because she has no place, no identity, nothing is fixed for her. As Madeline Moore notes, "Everything is an analogy, a symbol for something else. . . . Rhoda's apparently flexible imagination glosses over her selflessness; she can only liken herself to something else" (138). In contrast, Jinny and Susan have identities because they are able to insert themselves into society in culturally meaningful ways. Susan and Jinny are connected to the world not by what they do so much as by what they *are*. They assume identities made legitimate by the male system of representation: Susan is the maternal body, Jinny the sexual. The two are split to represent conventional, even stereotypical female ways of being in the world (as men have constructed those representations). Both act on desires produced, endorsed, and valued by the normative culture. Their desires are structured according to society's heterosexual imperative. Both orient themselves in relation to men and seek a generalized masculine approval. Susan shapes her identity by becoming maternal. Jinny's attention to her body provides the link with the world and sense of self-containment that Rhoda lacks. Both Susan and Jinny seem, for the most part, content with their choices.

If Rhoda is alienated from language and understanding, though, she is equally alienated from her body. As Louis remarks, "She has no body as the others have" (22). Or, in Rhoda's own words, "I am not here. I have no face. Other people have faces; Susan and Jinny have faces; they are here. Their world is the real world. The things they lift are heavy" (43). It is this uneasy combination that makes her so vulnerable, for while Bernard connects himself to the world with words and work and Jinny with the body, Rhoda has no means of connecting. Rhoda's disengaged, disembodied experience in the world suggests someone who has suffered a severe trauma and is too afraid to speak out or represent the experience.

However different from the others they may be, Louis and Rhoda are not judged or categorized, as Bernard's ambivalent feelings illustrate: "Louis, the attic dweller; Rhoda, the nymph of the fountain always wet, both contradicted what was then so positive to me; both gave the other side of what seemed to me so evident (that we marry, that we domesticate); for which I loved them, pitied them, and also deeply envied them their different lot" (259). For Bernard, Rhoda and Louis represent attractive alternatives to blind conventionality, ways of living that contradict what seems both positive and self-evident. Bernard does not objectify Rhoda as radically other than himself—as Jacques Hold will exclude and thus define Lol V. Stein—or as a construction of his own desires—as Nora Flood will construct Robin Vote in *Nightwood*. Bernard accepts the fact that a part of him is as much like Rhoda as any other figure but does not reduce her to himself. He accepts her difference. Through Bernard and the other speakers, Woolf does not exclude otherness or difference; her values are more inclusionary than exclusionary. Yet if Rhoda's marginality makes her compelling, she is also terrifying, for she exists in the space between sanity and madness, identity and personal disintegration.

If Rhoda and Louis contradict what seems self-evident to Bernard because they are not conventional, his "deep envy" of their difference camouflages the pain of their experience of exclusion. Since Bernard has the last word in the text—he speaks the entire last section—his perspective carries rhetorical weight and diffuses the suffering of the others; he turns the results of such pain into something to be envied. It's true that from his point of view Louis and Rhoda seem to escape the normalizing impulses of culture, but in another sense they do not. They are as much produced by their culture as the others. It is finally, as Madeline Moore states, "impossible to ignore the fact that Rhoda's and Louis's overwhelming longing for community is unfulfilled" (142). Bernard's response is complex and contradictory, indicative of the text's overall ambivalence, its desire to submerge consciousness in sensuous, aesthetic qualities while it insists on the effects of inequality and exclusion.

The Waves displays a desire for change and for pre-Oedipal union and connection—as in the moments when the speakers merge—as well as for difference and separation. The images of the waves throughout the different times of day that separate the sections in the text speak to such a desire for unity, for a natural but mystical wholeness. It is a desire most fragile, its object only partially achieved and then only for fleeting moments. It is a nostalgic desire, which intimates that connection and community might occur magically and internally, according to one's own subjective experience rather than through action or involvement in the world. Such a desire works to absorb the material differences of specific social and historical situations.

And yet material differences remain, particularly in individual subjective experiences. These experiences are distinct. If the image of the waves connotes mystical connection, the image of the willow tree reinforces radical separation. The sight of the willow triggers Neville's exuberant rapture, whereas for Rhoda it grows "on the verge of a grey desert where no bird sang" (252). It makes Bernard think how strange it looks when seen by each person in the group simultaneously. The resulting combination of impressions puts his imagination "under the compulsion of [the group's] clarity" (83). Although here the different versions of reality do not compete with one another, the differences challenge the authority of Bernard's own vision. In this text, no single view can be privileged over others.

The Waves produces representations of subjectivity and the world that depart in radical ways from conventional fictional forms. Because no one view or perspective is privileged, domination is refused. And yet it is only partially refused, since traces of injustice and profound difference remain. Oppression, Woolf implies in this text, cannot be resisted at the individual level. So even in her least overtly political novel, Woolf does not keep politics out of her work. However, in her last novel, *Between the Acts*, Woolf finds a new way to negotiate the conflicting claims of art and politics. *Between the Acts* is one of Woolf's most political texts, and yet, even here, the political critique is submerged to a great extent. In *Between the Acts*, Woolf moves away from the absorbing rhythm of *The Waves*

and, albeit more by juxtaposition and allusion than by explicit statement, makes a more overt critique of the violence of the patriarchal
household, women's vulnerability in society, and the exclusion of
women writers from literary history.

Recent feminist work on *Between the Acts* has focused on the
ways Woolf's feminism is encoded between the lines of the text, but
it has not stressed the relationship of this encoding to Woolf's ambivalence.[16] The feminist encoding occurs, for instance, in Bart
Oliver's quote from Swinburne's *Itylus*: "O sister swallow, O sister
swallow / How can thy heart be full of the Spring?" (115). In "Liberty, Sorority, Misogyny," Jane Marcus argues that "Woolf rewrites
[Swinburne's *Itylus*] in order to straighten out priorities. *Between
the Acts* tells us that 'what we must remember' is the rape; 'what
we must forget' is the male rewriting of women's history" (76). In
the original myth, Procne is given by her father to Tereus, king of
Thrace, who has assisted him in making war on the king of Thebes.
Procne bears Tereus a son, Itys. But Tereus falls in love with
Procne's sister, Philomela, whom he rapes. Fearing that she will
reveal the crime, he cuts out her tongue. Philomela is able to tell
Procne what happened by embroidering her story on a tapestry.
Overcome with rage, Procne kills her son Itys and serves him to his
father for dinner. She flees with Philomela, pursued by Tereus. A
god intervenes and turns Tereus into a hoopoe, Procne into a swallow, and Philomela into a nightingale. Itys is brought back to life
and changed into a goldfinch.[17] Marcus points out that Woolf "rejects Swinburne's recasting of the swallow and nightingale myth
from its original claim of the power of sisterhood over the patriarchal family to a misogynist nagging whine intended to produce
guilt" (76). In Swinburne's rewriting, the nightingale castigates her
sister for not feeling guilty about the murder of Itys. His nightingale forgets her rape, focusing instead on her fear that "the world
will end" if the murder of the male child is forgotten. She speaks
not of her own suffering—it can be forgotten and the world will
go on—but in support of male privilege. Women should remain silent, Swinburne has her imply, so that the world as it exists can
continue.

In the context of *Between the Acts* and Woolf's own struggles to
cross the boundaries of what she felt "permitted to say," this silence
is revealing. If indeed one feels that "the world will end" if one
speaks in ways that subvert male prerogative, one might choose, as

the nightingale in Swinburne's poem does, to remain silent, to re-press one's own rage. The known, however oppressive, can seem preferable to the terrors of the unknown—and if those terrors are emphasized, women can be made to support what oppresses them.

Woolf's rewriting of Swinburne's rewriting of the myth suggests her sense of her own vulnerability in speaking certain kinds of truths in her fiction. Woolf's message is encoded in the text—as Philomela's is embroidered into the tapestry and Miss La Trobe's is situated in and between the drama of her pageant—situated so as to slip past those figures who threaten, who, like Tereus and the soldiers Isa reads about in the newspaper, rape women and violate their ways of being in the world. All three must develop strategies for expression despite the constraints they face as women, whether they have been silenced like Philomela or through some of the more subtle ways women learn and internalize the belief that it is dan-gerous—even fatal—to speak openly of their experiences, their truths, for the world is filled with hostile, threatening, violent fig-ures. And yet, if encoded, the strategies one develops may not suc-ceed. La Trobe's play "fails" in the sense that it baffles her audience: they do not understand her meaning. Similarly, Woolf suggests her sense of her own failure to reach other women, who must read care-fully and between the lines.

Between the Acts rejects the patriarchal, imperialistic culture of the West and resists imagining the destruction of that culture. As Marilyn Brownstein notes, the text's relationship to culture is am-bivalent. Brownstein argues that desire emerges as an organizing principle, and in this she echoes Roland Barthes in *The Pleasure of the Text*: "Neither culture nor its destruction is erotic; it is the seam between them, the fault, the flaw which becomes so" (7). Brown-stein is right to point out that desire (in a psychoanalytic, not sexual, sense) is an organizing principle in *Between the Acts*. But Brownstein does not situate her analysis within a feminist perspec-tive, and Woolf's feminism is particularly significant in this text. Feminist readings tend to view the prehistoric allusions as indica-tive of prepatriarchal, matriarchal cultures or social arrangements, not as suggestions of the destruction of culture altogether.[18] I situ-ate myself between these approaches, for if Woolf wants to imagine a prepatriarchal social arrangement, she is only partially successful because at the same time she rejects such thinking as utopian fan-tasy. She uses the idea of the prehistoric to suggest what exceeds culture and resists absorption into any social arrangement or conceptual framework. Yet she is unwilling to pursue the destruction of culture: given the very real vulnerability of women in the world, it is hard to be unambivalent about what such destruction would mean for women. Speaking out about what one has learned to repress is threatening since it could bring about retribution or destroy the status quo. But if the existing culture is brutal to women, no culture at all, given the "unheard rhythms of [our] own wild hearts," might be even worse.

The desire for the destruction of patriarchal culture corresponds to a nostalgic longing for the imagined unity and safety one had with the mother before the entry into culture, for the pre-Oedipal experience precedes the moment of original loss. In *Between the Acts*, such longing is "sounded" and reenacted rather than represented: it is produced with preverbal feelings and images. Desire and loss are signaled most powerfully by the nonverbal, even the nonhuman. In the final scenes the sounds the cows make eclipse the human activity and accomplishment of the drama. In a strange sense, these animals express most fully human grief. Such grief cannot be put into words, it can only be sounded, much in the way that at the end of Faulkner's *The Sound and the Fury* Benjy Compson can only bellow. *Between the Acts* ends with a juxtaposition of Joseph Conrad and Matthew Arnold ("in the heart of darkness, in the fields of night" [219]). Language fails, as it failed Conrad's Marlow, who, having come up against the edge of the abyss where meaning is utterly undone, felt his failure lay in his inability to say anything about it.

In *Between the Acts*, Woolf comments only between the lines of the plot, through indirection. This commentary is self-conscious: Woolf suggests her assessment of her failure to cross the boundaries necessary as a woman writer to represent fully the unconscious, desire, sexuality, and the ways female subjectivities are produced within culture. These boundaries kept certain subjects— politics, her experience of her body, and incest—out of her fiction.

Woolf's encoding of incest in *Between the Acts* is especially revealing. In *Between the Acts* and its earlier version, *Pointz Hall*, Woolf moves toward finding a fictional form capable of representing incest. That she submerges the incest narrative to the extent that she does indicates, perhaps, her conviction that this was a subject she should not explore—especially as a woman and a victim of incest herself—in her art. It is, however, appropriate that the incest narrative is implied in a text concerned with culture and its destruction, the brutality of the patriarchal household, and an artist's sense of her own failure. It is also fitting that Woolf should address this subject at roughly the same time she took it up in terms of her own childhood experience with Gerald Duckworth in "A Sketch of the Past."

The form of incest Woolf portrays in *Between the Acts* parallels her own experience in several ways. It occurs between a brother and sister, with the brother holding considerable power in relation to his sister. Moreover, in the early version of *Pointz Hall*, Lucy's father purchases the paintings of the ancestors, which suggests that, like Woolf and her half brothers, Lucy and Bart had different fathers. (In the later text, Bart purchases the paintings.) In addition, *Pointz Hall* ends with the image of Lucy and Bart going upstairs together to bed, like an old married couple—in "22 Hyde Park Gate" it is after Woolf has gone to bed that George comes and flings himself on her.

With this final image of Bart and Lucy going upstairs to bed, Lucy's earlier remarks to William Dodge (which exist in both early and later versions of *Pointz Hall*) when she shows him the house are more suggestive. She says to Dodge: "'Up and up they went' . . . seeing, it seemed, an invisible procession, 'up and up to bed' . . . 'I ignore. I forget'"(69). What she remembers is unclear and actually seems to be a collage of different events, some of which she would rather ignore or forget. She stops at a bedroom door, tapping "twice very distinctly" (69). She listens. "'One never knows,' she murmured, 'if there's somebody there'" (69). Woolf makes clear in what follows that William, although he senses the depth of Lucy's pain, does not understand her reactions or comments. When she sinks down on the edge of the bed he thinks it is because she is tired, "no doubt, by the stairs, by the heat" (70). However, by adding "no doubt," Woolf actually produces doubt in the reader's mind, implying that it is something more than the stairs and the heat that causes Lucy's sudden exhaustion. As if rejecting her own past, Lucy murmurs, "But we have other lives, I think, I hope. . . . We live in others, Mr. . . . We live in things" (70). Often interpreted as part of Woolf's more general understanding of subjectivity, these words, spoken in this context, also point toward Lucy's desire to escape the weight of her own particular past. If William does not understand the source of Lucy's pain, his response is immediate and sympathetic, translating her pain into a similar experience of his own that he is unable to express: "He wished to kneel before her, to kiss her hand, and to say: 'At school they held me under a bucket of dirty water, Mrs. Swithin; when I looked up, the world was dirty, Mrs. Swithin; so I married; but my child's not my child, Mrs. Swithin. I'm a half-man, Mrs. Swithin; a flickering, mind-divided little snake in the grass, Mrs. Swithin . . .' So he wished to say; but said nothing . . ." (73).

Later, in a scene that recalls Lucy's ritualized appearance at the bedroom door with William Dodge, Lucy appears on another threshold. This time it is at the entrance to a room where her brother sits alone with his dog, muttering "O sister swallow, O sister swallow": "The door trembled and stood half open. That was Lucy's way of coming in—as if she did not know what she would find. Really! It was her brother!" (116) In contrast to the way Woolf writes publicly about her response to George Duckworth's unwanted attentions, Lucy seems a much more willing participant. Woolf hints that Lucy knows—perhaps has always known—when and where she would find her brother. Lucy perches on the edge of a chair, and Bart's words change slightly but significantly: "Swallow, my sister, O sister swallow . . ." (116). As Mitchell Leaska writes, "It is just possible that [Woolf] meant the word 'swallow' also to be read as the imperative form of the verb, thereby introducing considerable irony into this already sexually-charged Swinburne allusion" (220).

Madeline Moore comments that in *Between the Acts* Woolf shifts the focus of her mythic framework from the Demeter-Persephone myth of her earlier fiction, which promises that the mother will search for the daughter and deliver her from rape and heterosexual violence, thus insisting on community among women, to the myth of Isis and Osiris, which involves a marriage between a brother and sister: "This shift tells us almost everything about the novel" (156). And it is compatible with the warning in Swinburne's rewriting of the Procne-Philomela myth, for the Isis-Osiris myth is a story of wifely heroism rather than of female bonding and defiance.[19] In the myth, Isis marries her brother Osiris and helps him rule Egypt. When Osiris is assassinated by their brother Set, Isis recovers the body. But Set recaptures it, cuts it into fourteen pieces, and scatters them. Then Isis searches until she finds all the fragments but one—the phallus, which has been eaten by a crab. Isis reconstitutes her brother/husband's body (minus the phallus) and performs rites of embalmment that restore Osiris to eternal life. Moore notes that for her accomplishment Isis was considered a magician and adds that, like Isis, Woolf "was trying to regather the fragments of English literature/culture into such a form as to make it palatable to women and their working-class brothers" (156). This may be, but in order to read between the lines of *Between the Acts* one must be an educated reader: this is not a text to appeal to a wide readership. The reader must work hard, like Isis, piecing together the scattered fragments of this textual body to guarantee meaning. And, of course, at another level the Isis-Osiris myth provides a commentary on the relationship between Lucy and Bart.

The phallus is, however, very much intact in this text, for *Between the Acts* reveals how social and material forces keep gender divisions distinct and in place. Woolf represents such forces as inseparable from brutality, militarism, oppressive economic systems, and imperialism. Lucy Swithin and Isa Oliver live like inmates in the patriarchal house of Bart Oliver, Lucy's brother and Isa's father-in-law. The house, according to Bart, was built in order to "escape from nature" (8), which, given the cultural correlation between woman and nature, underscores that it is a place of male bonding, masculine values, and patriarchal authority. Accordingly, the house is a place where Lucy often seems rather silly and out of place and where Isa must hide what she writes in a "book bound like an account book in case Giles suspected" that she was writing more personal impressions, feelings, and thoughts (15). It is a place where a woman is said to have killed herself.

Lucy's and Isa's relationships to the house and what it represents are ambivalent. Marginal because female, they are still relatively dominant figures because of the social ties binding them to their male counterparts. Lucy is, like Isis to Osiris, intimately connected to her brother Bart. If their relationship is incestuous, it is also true that "nothing changed their affection; no argument; no fact; no truth" (26). Radically different from one another, they are also aligned with one another. Lucy participates in her own oppression, even while her interest in prehistory suggests her resistance. As Giles's wife, Isa (whose name evokes Isis) occupies a privileged and protected position. But her Irish descent displays her difference from British military and economic imperialism: she is colonized as well as complicit with respect to both gender and ethnicity.

Bart Oliver, formerly of the British Indian Civil Service, expresses values both masculine and imperialist. In his house connections to military life are maintained, even enshrined: the "butler had been a soldier . . . and, under a glass case there was a watch that had stopped a bullet on the field of Waterloo" (7). In order to acquire significance, local events, such as the discussion of where to put the town's cesspool, are put within the context of Bart's knowledge of military history. Bart notes that from the air, the site they had chosen for the cesspool was plainly marked with "the scars made by the Britons; by the Romans; by the Elizabethan manor house; and by the plough, when they ploughed the hill to grow wheat in the Napoleonic wars" (4).

But these "scars" signify more than Bart intends. Not only do they equate military history with a cesspool, they reverberate with the account of the rape Isa reads in the paper:

> For her generation the newspaper was a book; and, as her father-in-law had dropped the *Times*, she took it and read: "A horse with a green tail . . ." which was fantastic. Next, "The guard at Whitehall . . ." which was romantic, and then, building word upon word, she read: "The troopers told her the horse had a green tail; but she found it was just an ordinary horse. And they dragged her up to a barrack room where she was thrown upon a bed. Then one of the troopers removed part of her clothing, and she screamed and hit him about the face." (20)

Isa's experience parallels the victim's: initially she too is seduced by the fantastical, romantic language in the paper—until the brutal reality of what she is reading hits her. Because the newspaper moves from Bart to Isa, he is connected with both the article and the language. Not only is he connected through physical and temporal proximity, he was himself a trooper, a military man, like those who do the raping. Isa, on the other hand, identifies strongly with the woman. She is unable to forget what she has read, while Bart drops the paper, seemingly unaffected by it.

Even though Woolf implies Lucy has consented to an incestuous relationship with Bart and participated in her own oppression, Lucy is at the same time a victim. She and the woman who is raped are intimately connected to one another. Immediately after Isa reads of the rape, Lucy comes into the room carrying a hammer. When a few pages later Isa recalls the image of the woman being attacked, in her mind that woman attempts to protect herself by screaming and striking her attacker about the face with a hammer. But there is no mention of a hammer in the first passage. Thus, for Isa, Lucy becomes identified with the victim of the attack, while Bart, who keeps thinking of Byron (who also had an incestuous relationship with his half sister), is identified with the attackers. Woolf intimates that at some level Isa is aware of their illicit relationship. Since Lucy has not aggressively challenged her oppression and Isa has not come to her defense, they are perhaps complicit in what goes on. But they are not oppressors themselves. Moreover, this identification of Lucy as victim makes the passage between the moment when Isa reads of the rape and when she imagines the woman protecting herself with a hammer especially evocative. Between these passages Woolf inserts a seemingly innocent memory of Lucy and Bart going fishing. The memory becomes, in this context, sexually suggestive and violent: "Once, she remembered, he had made her take the fish off the hook herself. The blood had shocked her—'Oh!' she had cried, for the gills were full of blood. And he had growled: 'Cindy!' The ghost of that morning in the meadow was in her mind as she replaced the hammer" (21).

Both Bart and Giles Oliver bring a form of masculine brutality into the house, and their violence signals profound male bonding and the conditions of that bonding. Bart treats his Afghan hound Sohrab in such a way that the dog "never admitted the ties of domesticity. Either he cringed or he bit" (18). Bart springs upon his grandson George, who, interrupted in his exploration of the garden, topples over in fright to see the "terrible peaked eyeless monster" that is his grandfather (11–12). Meanwhile Sohrab is bounding among the flowers, destroying the garden: "'Heel!' the old man bawled, as if he were commanding a regiment. It was impressive, to the nurses, the way an old boy of his age could still bawl and make a brute like that obey him. Back came the Afghan hound, sidling, apologetic. And as he cringed at the old man's feet, a string was slipped over his collar; the noose that old Oliver always carried with him" (12). It isn't until Oliver has restrained the dog with this noose that George begins to cry, only to have his grandfather dismiss him as a crybaby and walk away. Bart finds this response inappropriate for a boy and makes a point of letting Isa know it.

But George's response is eminently reasonable. The name Sohrab recalls Matthew Arnold's poem "Sohrab and Rustum," inspired by the story of the father and son in Sir John Malcolm's *History of Persia*. In Arnold's poem, as in the story and as in the myth of Procne and Philomela, a king gives his daughter as a gift to one of his friends—in this case to Rustum, his "wandering friend" whom he loves well. There's no question of marriage—it's an arrangement between the two men. After Rustum leaves, however, the king's daughter bears a son. She sends word that it is a "puny girl, no boy at all" (609) for fear that "Rustum should seek the boy, to train in arms" (611). Her attempt to save her son from war and violence fails: Sohrab does go to war when he's grown. And he seeks a military career in order that he may both prove himself to his unknown father by reputation and perhaps find him as well, since his father is also a commander. When they do meet, as of course they must, neither knows the other's identity. They fight, and in the course of the struggle (in an Oedipal reversal) Rustum kills Sohrab, only to learn that the daughter he thought he had is a son—and that he has just killed him.

The poem suggests the symbolic importance of the bond between father and son, its complexities, and its basis in faith (unlike the maternal bond, which, because women give birth, is undeniable). It shows the dangers of war, violence, and masculine forms of brutality that threaten both men and women. If the kinship between Sohrab and Rustum is disguised, it is nevertheless there. Each man who dies in battle is someone's son. The poem anxiously insists that it is male kinship that counts. Women are devalued throughout, ostensibly because they do not fight and, more to the point, because they are excluded from male cultural bonding. ("For would that I myself had such a son, / And not that one slight helpless girl I have—" [229–230]; "I am no girl, to be made pale by words" [381].) In this context, George just doesn't measure up (at least not yet): he is not the kind of son these fathers wish for.

This privileging of male community and masculine values is homoerotic. The real bonds exist between men, calling into question and contradicting the official cultural story of heterosexuality. Women exist for men: they can be exchanged between male friends or they can be seized as trophies of war. Armies of men united in violence are socially legitimate, even honored. But the official ideology has no tolerance for and will not recognize men who do not repress their attraction to other men.

In contrast to Bart's brutality and Giles's conventional brand of

masculinity, William Dodge is gentle, unthreatening, and homosexual. He represents perversion to a culture dominated by males
whose energies are spent denying that their deepest bonds are with
other men. In a gesture of stamping out such "unnatural" inversions and perversions, Giles smashes with his foot a snake that is
unable to swallow a frog. The action—the fact of taking some kind
of action—relieves him, convinces him that he is different from the
likes of William Dodge. He is normal, heterosexual, a lover of
women. William's difference from the masculine norm frees both
Isa and Mrs. Swithin to be at ease with him. But he suffers terribly.
He is a victim in at least two ways. First, he has been singled out by
the other children and tormented because he is different. ("At
school they held me under a bucket of dirty water, Mrs. Swithin;
when I looked up, the world was dirty, Mrs. Swithin" [73].) Second, like Louis, he has internalized a sense of what others have
defined as his inferiority. ("I'm a half-man, Mrs. Swithin; a flickering, mind-divided little snake in the grass, Mrs. Swithin; as Giles
saw" [73].)

Since William refers to himself as a little snake and Giles crushes
a snake underfoot, Giles's action testifies to his desire to crush William. He would stamp out William's difference, his "perversion." For
to Giles, William is "a toady; a lickspittle; not a downright plain man
of his senses; but a teaser and a twitcher; a fingerer of sensations;
picking and choosing; dillying and dallying; not a man to have
straightforward love for a woman . . . but simply a———At this
word, which he could not speak in public, he pursed his lips; and
the signet-ring on his little finger looked redder, for the flesh next
to it whitened as he gripped the arm of his chair" (60). Giles does
precisely what Woolf refuses to do. His ethic is based on exclusion
and judgment, hers is not. William is essentially a convenient peg
upon which Giles can hang his more generalized anger and frustration. In fact, by despising William he is able to keep from despising
himself. He takes refuge in conventions that become convenient
forms for hostility; he remains blind and ignorant, not only of William but of himself.

Each character, with the possible exception of La Trobe, is to a
great extent constrained by the parts society decides he or she must
play; if art imitates life, life also imitates art. As Patricia Waugh
argues, Woolf shows how self-representation is constructed from
available, contradictory discourses. This representation is deter-

mined by class, gender, ethnicity, and sexuality. Mrs. Manresa's vulgarity suggests she is a member of the new middle class: her money is new, not old. She presents herself as a "wild child of nature," and in a sense she is, but in another sense she is not—her wildness is an act designed to attract men (which it does: she doesn't act this way for nothing). It is all surface, though, revealing nothing of any truly untamed aspects of her subjectivity. Her so-called wildness is nothing if not tame: it is conventional female behavior, recognizable as artifice. As Marilyn Brownstein notes, "Mrs. Manresa's artistry in creating desire is a parody of the Romantic solution in that she is the object of all desiring on a summer day" (86). Because this identity is an artifice she maintains so conscientiously, unlike the others she is able to gaze directly into the mirrors held up to the audience at the end of the performance. While the others twist and squirm, self-conscious at being caught and exposed, Mrs. Manresa basks in her own reflection. As Eileen Barrett points out, "Mrs. Manresa springs Athena-like from the male mind. Her name, 'man' plus *res*, the Latin for thing, emphasizes her allegiances and establishes her as the image of the goddess in the male imagination" (24). A man's thing, she prefers men—"obviously" we are told (39). Referred to as "the Manresa" (110), she is herself an object, a performance.

Isa engages in performance as well. Even when she drops the part she plays in her daily life, she fashions for herself a part composed of both Juliet and Lady Macbeth: "'She spake,' Isa murmured. 'And from her bosom's snowy antre drew the gleaming blade. "Plunge blade!" she said. And struck. "Faithless!" she cried. Knife, too! It broke. So too my heart,' she said" (113). Her murderous impulses are interwoven with suicidal intentions. She directs her anger toward herself. That she chooses fragments of characters' lines as forms of expression makes clear the extent to which her avenues of action are charted by systems of representation. Isa acts a role that combines the self-sacrificing Juliet who cannot live without her lover and the scheming Lady Macbeth. While her anger is very real and subversive, her avenues of expression are constricted to constructions of women formed in the male imagination.

La Trobe is harder to place, for she does not act according to cultural representations of femininity. The townspeople don't know much about her and assume that with a name like La Trobe she isn't purely English. Some speculate that she has Russian blood or comes from the Channel Islands. It is known that she had been an actress and shared a cottage with another woman with whom she had quarreled. Because she strode through fields "sometimes with a cigarette in her mouth; often with a whip in her hand; and used rather strong language," she is suspected of not being "altogether a lady" (58). In any case, she is one of the strongest females in Woolf's fiction, neither flighty like Lucy nor a prisoner in anyone's home like Isa and not male-identified like Mrs. Manresa.

As the last female artist Woolf would portray, La Trobe seems particularly compelling, a later version of Lily Briscoe who, like Lily, struggles with her vision and, like Woolf after she completed a novel, struggles with depression. She believes her work ultimately fails: during the performance she suffers "triumph, humiliation, ecstasy, despair—for nothing" (210). Misunderstood by the rector, her work is incomprehensible or offensive to most of her audience. Like William she is marginalized and transgressive: as a lesbian she prefers women to men. Since breaking with "the actress who had shared her bed and her purse" (211), she has begun to drink excessively. She knows she's on the edge of society, just barely contained by its codes. With as much certainty as knowing she "would drop her suit case in at the kitchen window" on her way to the pub, she thinks that "one of these days she would break—which of the village laws? Sobriety? Chastity? Or take something that did not properly belong to her?" (211) She already breaks a number of conventions that govern female behavior. She loves other women, refuses to define herself in relation to men as does Manresa, has a passion for "getting things up," and expresses her anger more openly than any other female in Woolf's fiction. And yet she compromises too much: she is a slave to her audience. She cares too much what others think.

Woolf claimed that with *The Waves* she wanted to break through the surface of things into the depths of consciousness and personality, but she goes farthest with *Between the Acts*. *Between the Acts* considers the demonic, wild aspects of subjectivity more explicitly than Woolf's other fiction, for it points toward the extent to which we are "savages still" (199). Lucy Swithin, with her interest in prehistoric creatures (both human and nonhuman), rejects the idea of historical progress and change. She muses about Victorians: "I don't believe . . . that there ever were such people. Only you and me and William dressed differently" (174–175). The perspective the novel takes is more ambivalent, however; it is closer to Isa's response to Lucy's question as to whether we "act different parts but are the same": "'Yes,' Isa answered. 'No,' she added. It was Yes, No. Yes, yes, yes, the tide rushed out embracing. No, no, no, it contracted" (215). The text offers no definitive answers to the questions it raises: the responses are not yes *or* no but yes *and* no. That is to say, its structure is contradictory and ambivalent. Woolf wants to clear a space in which a new story could be told apart from centuries of patriarchal baggage, liberated from internalized constraints and fears. *Between the Acts* is her most painful book to read because it is a statement of her failure to accomplish as much as she had wished.

In contrast to Woolf's internalized constraints, the swallows dance to the "unheard rhythm of their own wild hearts" (65), recalling Procne, who was turned into a swallow and who did, in fact, follow such rhythms in revenging her sister's suffering, breaking a fundamental cultural taboo in murdering her own child. None of the characters in Woolf's fiction can hear such a rhythm. But to hear it is to hear a story that has not, Woolf implies, yet been written. The stage Woolf sets for this story is prehistoric: "It was night before roads were made, or houses. It was the night that dwellers in caves had watched from some high place among rocks" (219). And as Barrett notes, this moment "recalls the moment after the pageant when La Trobe, standing on the terrace, imagines her next play as a prehistoric scene" (35). "'I should group them,' she murmured, 'here.' It would be midnight; there would be two figures, half concealed by a rock. The curtain would rise" (210).

Barrett's point is that, rather than rewriting Genesis as Marcus suggests, La Trobe plans to stage a matriarchal play: "Her characters, perhaps, are the primitive celebrants who wait for Isa's release from the 'heart of darkness,' 'the fields of night,' to celebrate her springtime reunion with her mother/Goddess, her mythic origins, and to rewrite the plot . . . to prevent the rape" (35). But this reading dismisses the "heart of darkness" toward which this text moves a little too easily. The traces of desire in the writing represent the potential for the destruction of culture. The ending is far from utopian: it is not a matriarchal fantasy that Woolf indulges but a language that would write directly toward what culture represses, that would write of the night, of the unconscious, and of unexplored regions of female subjectivity.

When, in the final scene, the audience is suddenly caught un-awares by their own unguarded reflections, the rhythm they are accustomed to hearing suddenly "kicked, reared, [and] snapped short" (183). As the cows join in, the audience is unable to distin-guish themselves from the beasts: "Walloping, tail lashing, the reti-cence of nature was undone, and the barriers which should divide Man the Master from the Brute were dissolved" (184). All forms of human mastery are temporarily undone: the uproar is "quite be-yond control" (184). It is this realm, where Woolf never fully or unambivalently ventured, that Djuna Barnes maps in *Nightwood*.

3 Djuna Barnes and the Politics of the Night

For Virginia Woolf, rhythmic, lyrical prose was an ideal form. With such prose she could accomplish contradictory aims: she could write toward subjects she felt were transgressive, taboo, and dangerous (the force of the unconscious, women's experiences and vulnerability in the world, female desires and sexuality), while she could, with an aestheticizing diffuseness, retreat from some of the more frightening and violent aspects of subjectivity such explorations necessarily involve. She could put into her fiction a sense of the struggle between prosodic and symbolic properties in language—and in such a way as to suggest the force of a desire capable of destroying culture while achieving, paradoxically, in her own work a highly sophisticated form of cultural expression. She could reveal and conceal her subjects. By way of contrast, Djuna Barnes's *Nightwood*, although diffuse in the sense that it maps the irrational "night world," is anything but an aesthetic retreat from the violence of sexuality and desire. By delving into the "heart of darkness" without the limitations of the boundaries formed by Woolf's internalized restraints, Barnes produces a force fueled by conscious and unconscious desire, obsession, and violence. This force shatters any aestheticizing qualities characteristic of lyricism, though Barnes's work, like Woolf's, owes much of its intensity to contradictory impulses.

Nightwood maps regions of female subjectivity and desire much more explicitly than Woolf's fiction. Like Woolf, Barnes is interested in what has not been previously explored, but she takes the whole enterprise of mapping female subjectivity and desire further by writing directly of the power of unconscious forces in structuring desire. She uses desire as a force to exceed what is rational or contained. For Barnes, desire cannot be contained by definitions any more than it can be made to conform with socially legitimized ideals. Because to some extent demonic, it overturns such ideals and the discourses that sustain such ideals, including those with which Nora initially fashions herself. But Nora's way of seeing the world is severely curtailed and thus flawed, as we come to see given the ways *Nightwood* critiques and parodies the use of dominant discourses to territorialize and thus control feminine desire and subjectivity.

Nightwood shows that, inscribed by forms of power that structure society and sexuality, desire is formed in relation to and yet always exceeds such powers, including psychoanalysis, religion, ideas of what constitutes gendered subjects and gendered behavior, and institutionalized heterosexuality. It resists imperialistic discourses and impulses by refusing formulas or simplistic, reductive categories of human subjects; it subverts the powers that operate by classifying human subjects and experiences in order to define and privilege certain configurations of health, sexuality, gender, ethnicity, or religion. For all these reasons, the text is deeply disturbing. But even more unsettling are the ways the text seems strangely in collusion with what it ostensibly critiques. *Nightwood* takes shape along contradictory lines: not only does its fantastical prose explode dominant discourses with the force of desire, it to some extent reinscribes key components of fascistic discourses. The text's language seems at once subversive and complicit, comic and tragic, sexist and feminist, racist and not racist, ahistorical and historical. Cannot, Matthew asks, "a beastly thing be analogous to a fine thing if both are apprehensions?" (125). It would seem so: in *Nightwood* such oppositions collapse, producing a fearful force of unusual intensity.

While Barnes was more open than Woolf with respect to transgressive subjects, she was not free from all constraints. Whereas for the most part Woolf experienced what restrained her from writing what and as she liked as internal constrictions, the restraints Barnes experienced were largely external. She could and did write of the "night world" and the violence of desire as experienced by women. But unlike Woolf, she did not have the means to publish her own work. Her ostensible freedom was comparatively curtailed.

To a greater extent she simply *had* to care at some point what others, particularly publishers, thought. The story of *Nightwood*'s publication, a story of such restraints, is a tale of male power and prerogative, of masculine cultural authority. What we have to work with is, as a result, a problematic text.

In 1935, after a frustrating and unsuccessful attempt to find an American publisher (a period of time, in Andrew Field's words, when the manuscript "did not even suffer the usual agonizing delays but shot in and out of the publishers' offices as though it were being ejected from a greased revolving door in an old silent movie" [207]), Barnes's manuscript reached T. S. Eliot at Faber and Faber in London. Like some of the American editors, Eliot told Barnes that in order for the manuscript to be published sections would have to be cut. So Barnes gave Eliot the freedom to edit as he wished. Critics report variously about the extent to which he exercised this privilege. Field claims Barnes had written 190,000 words and that she herself cut it to 65,000 before the manuscript reached Eliot. (The published version is roughly 50,000 words.) According to Field, Eliot "concentrated mainly on paring down the part of the doctor who he was anxious should not be allowed to steal the main attention in the novel" (212). But recent feminist analyses interpret the evidence in Barnes's manuscripts differently. Shari Benstock claims Eliot reduced the manuscript by more than two-thirds and eliminated—"among other things—scenes that expressed explicit lesbian rage and virulent anticlerical sentiment" (428).[1] If the extent of Eliot's role is for the moment somewhat controversial, even mysterious, still it is certain that he influenced the final form of Barnes's major literary text.[2]

The title *Nightwood* was Eliot's idea. It is a rich and resonant title for this text, and Barnes apparently accepted it quickly and easily. As Field points out, it is easy to imagine Barnes's delight at Eliot's proposal "with its unwitting secret watermark of Thelma's name in it" (212). For it has been supposed by many that Thelma Wood, Barnes's lover in Paris, inspired the fictional figure of Robin Vote, the strange, nocturnal, and haunting presence around which other figures circulate.[3] At the same time, *Nightwood* suggests Nora Flood: in her "there could be seen coming, early in her life, the design that was to be the weather-beaten grain of her face, that wood in the work; the tree coming forward in her, an undocumented record of time" (50). The title thus links Nora and Robin, who are in fact intimately connected since, for Nora, Robin comes to symbolize her own unacknowledged and unconscious desires.

In yet another sense the title resonates with the Night Town episode in Joyce's *Ulysses*, for *Nightwood* rewrites Night Town's withdrawal of rationality. Leopold Bloom's experience in Night Town is episodic—it's just a temporary excursion into the world of the night; Bloom returns to the rational world empowered and renewed by his experience. *Nightwood*'s withdrawal from rationality is not episodic but virtually entire: it ventures further away from the meaningful constructs of culture throughout the entire text. But however appropriate the title, a feminist critic is likely to feel, as I do, somewhat uneasy about Eliot's involvement with *Nightwood*. Although he and Barnes maintained a connection over the years following its publication and although he admired *Nightwood* more and more, as Jane Marcus puts it, "Like Djuna herself, [one] feels ambivalent about Eliot's role in her life, and has a perverse desire to see the publication of the whole manuscript of *Nightwood*, to find out what it was like before the editorial red pencils cut it down to size" ("Carnival" 6).[4]

The story of *Nightwood*'s publication reads as Barnes's struggle to have her expression made public against considerable odds. Likewise, the text itself maps Nora's fight to find her own voice despite all the forces, including social and cultural conditions, that conspire to prevent her from finding it. Nora's love for Robin, a woman who is both different from and the same as herself, is intimately connected to her effort to articulate and know herself in ways not previously charted by culture or in its texts. A product of an American heritage and its puritanical values, Nora admits only to rational qualities, which, in combination with her attempts at self-justification, make her largely unknown to herself. We are all, to some extent, unknown to ourselves: *Nightwood* writes toward this unknown, toward those aspects of ourselves that we cannot know because they cannot be put into language or given a final, fixed form. But Nora's situation is different, for a woman who loves and desires another woman would not, especially in the early twentieth century, find many cultural texts or artifacts to help her articulate her own experience and difference from the heterosexual norm.

Given Nora's struggle to articulate her own version of her identity and experience and to speak of these things to Matthew O'Connor, a male whose compulsive need to speak is overwhelming and often threatens to drown Nora's voice entirely, Eliot's influential involvement with *Nightwood*'s publication seems eerily prefigured in the text itself. That is the case, however, with an important qualification: Matthew's authority is effectively undermined, whereas Eliot's authority to determine the shape of *Nightwood* was definitive. Matthew does not prevent Nora from speaking her own truths. Little about Matthew is legitimate or powerful, though he is sought after by the marginal figures in the text. In contrast, Eliot was a person of considerable influence and cultural power. We read Eliot's edited version, and some even argue that it is only owing to Eliot's endorsement that Barnes's work is recognized at all.

Many voices speak in *Nightwood*, undermining the authority of any one position and producing a contradictory and heterogeneous discourse composed of an amalgam of styles and perspectives. Some are fascistic, some are not. What Jane Marcus has called its "carnival of voices" represents the strength of social authority as well as resistance to it, the constructed nature of that authority along with the desire for a more authentic "natural" authority, and subjects produced by and in social configurations in such ways that they resist and desire their own captivity, subjection, and purification. That is to say, they perpetuate and thus are in collusion with structures that produce dominance and subordination. Whereas on the one hand *Nightwood* undermines social control in order to produce a textual terrain relatively free from constraint, on the other the figures who populate this terrain are anything but free from a will to power: they want to constrain or control others—or to be controlled themselves. This radical split runs throughout the text like a geological fault line under its performative surface.

Nora is a good example of this contradictory split, for she is in collusion with the repressive structures she ostensibly opposes. She wants power, but when she goes to Matthew to learn of the night, for she has been unwilling or unable to risk experiencing it directly, she grants him what the text denies him: the authority of a doctor, priest, or prophet. Her intent is self-serving. She wants him to somehow validate the unique intensity of her own pain, as well as her desire to set limits on Robin (who mirrors unacknowledged parts of herself), in ways that will return power to herself. Her will is voracious. She insists upon the difference of her relationship with

Robin, and yet she perpetuates heterosexual structures and ways of being in that relationship. She wants to control Robin, to possess her. She wants to believe they are precisely the same, even as she recognizes their differences.

Robin too is contradictory. Although she rejects Nora's possessiveness, she also wants to be protected by Nora's love, as is illustrated when she pleads, "You have got to stay with me or I can't live" (143). To some extent complicit with the possessive mechanisms operating between them, Robin also wants to destroy these mechanisms in order to be "free." When Nora tries to keep strangers' hands off Robin, Robin lashes out at her, running behind her for blocks accusing "with a furious panting breath, 'You are a devil! You make everything dirty! . . . You make me feel dirty and tired and old'" (143).

With Robin, Barnes provides an alternate way of seeing Nora's puritanical and controlling impulses and finds a way to symbolize what exists beyond a culture that produces subjects so desperate and needy. This antithesis to culture, Barnes seems to suggest by linking Robin with both, is our future as well as our past. What makes Robin such a haunting and terrifying figure is that she embodies the antithesis of culture. Although she keeps "repeating in one way or another her wish for a home" (55), she cannot stay fixed within the confining architecture of any cultural construct. Perhaps she seems very much "alive" because always moving and compelling because she moves at the very limits of what the other characters dare to imagine, but she is tormented, an alarming creature who, because racked with pain, "sleepwalks" through life so that she will only half suffer.

Nora's life with Robin provides a temporary and tenuous escape from society and thus from history, which is impossible to escape absolutely or authentically. But for a time she is able to withdraw from the world into the more thrilling private place they construct together. This private world, like the text itself, is filled with signs of theater and spectacle: "circus chairs, wooden horses bought from a ring of an old merry-go-round, venetian chandeliers from the Flea Fair, stage-drops from Munich, cherubim from Vienna, ecclesiastical hangings from Rome, a spinet from England, and a miscellaneous collection of music boxes from many countries" (55–56). Their home is fantastical, eccentric, and theatrical, thrilling in its difference. These theatrical accoutrements and circus props indicate that their life together is all at once an escape from history, a retreat from life into art, something of a dramatic performance, and a struggle to find a new form for a new relationship. Robin's speech is also linked with dramatic performance: "In the tones of this girl's voice was the pitch of one enchanted with the gift of postponed abandon: the low drawling 'aside' voice of the actor who, in the soft usury of his speech, withholds a vocabulary until the profitable moment when he shall be facing his audience" (38). The language is highly stylized and theatrical: Robin is described as "enchanted with the gift of postponed abandon" (38), a curious way to suggest that she withholds conversation and connection. Robin stages herself and keeps herself from being known apart from the way she chooses to present herself. The theatricality implies mystery, because what lies beyond Robin's guarded persona is unknown.

Like the house that Robin and Nora inhabit together and like Robin herself, the language of the text is theatrical, a performance. Robin and Nora's ambivalent relation to history and society is mirrored by the language of the text, which shares in the desire to be free from confinement. It frees customary symbolic restraints as it points toward the unknown. By fracturing syntax and sense it produces a certain intuitive but not literal sense. The language follows not *a* rhythm but many rhythms. It shapes without entirely containing its subject, as in the following passage describing Robin:

> The woman who presents herself to the spectator as a "picture" forever arranged is, for the contemplative mind, the chiefest danger. Sometimes one meets a woman who is beast turning human. Such a person's every movement will reduce to an image of a forgotten experience; a mirage of an eternal wedding cast on the racial memory; as insupportable a joy as would be the vision of an eland coming down an aisle of trees, chapleted with orange blossoms and a bridal veil, a hoof raised in the economy of fear, stepping in the trepidation of flesh that will become myth; as the unicorn is neither man nor beast deprived, but human hunger pressing its breast to its prey.
>
> Such a woman is the infected carrier of the past: before her the structure of our head and jaws ache—we feel that we could eat her, she who is eaten death returning, for only then do we put our face close to the blood on the lips of our forefathers. (37)

The passage begins by stating that the woman who turns herself into an image to be contemplated is the chief danger, but rather than explaining or elaborating this idea, it jumps to the very different idea of "beast turning human." A reader is immediately thrown off balance. The rest of the paragraph accumulates clauses without any kind of break. The effect is as disconcerting as the images described: "a mirage of an eternal wedding"; a cannibalism that includes us—"we feel that we could eat her"—collapses the structures of culture that separate us from prehistory. It is not possible, Barnes suggests, to be radically different from our "barbarian" ancestors. Barnes challenges our sense of ourselves as rational individuals in the world, for the beast forces the retreat of both rationality and individuality. To deny this is to be like Nora, who is blind to the beast in herself but can sense it in Robin. And Barnes's point is more ahistorical than historical: this desire to "put our face close to the blood on the lips of our forefathers" transcends space and time. It is not explicitly linked to a particular historical context; its danger (arrived at through women like Robin) is universal.

In the final chapter, it is the language as much as it is what actually happens that gives the encounter between Robin and Nora's dog sexual overtones and thus positions it absolutely outside "normal" human behavior, producing a spectacle of transgression. More precisely, it is the rhythm of the language, which quickens with increasing intensity as Robin "goes down" in the chapel, approaches the dog, and, worse, against its will backs it into a corner:

> Then she began to bark also, crawling after him--barking in
> a fit of laughter, obscene and touching. The dog began to cry
> then, running with her, head-on with her head, as if to circum-
> vent her; soft and slow his feet went padding. He ran this way
> and that, low down in his throat crying, and she grinning and
> crying with him; crying in shorter and shorter spaces, moving
> head to head, until she gave up, lying out, her hands beside
> her, her face turned and weeping; and the dog too gave up
> then, and lay down, his eyes bloodshot, his head flat along her
> knees. (170)

This prose depends upon and foregrounds rhythm and cadence: these nonsignifying properties, paradoxically enough, *do* signify. As the passage describes "shorter and shorter spaces" so too do its own clauses become shorter and shorter to produce a sense of sexual intensity. What occurs between Robin and the dog is alarming, frightening, a spectacle produced by a warp in the representational fabric of language.

With all its theatricality, language offers in *Nightwood* the alluring if ultimately illusive possibility of an escape from the materiality of history. This is one of the central contradictions that runs
through *Nightwood*, cutting across a number of fields. Barnes's language may not offer the sometimes diffuse, aesthetic retreat of Virginia Woolf's, but it offers a different kind of escape into a spectacular shattering of discourse that is at once theatrical, performative,
comic, and alarming. Its theatricality produces a sense of a more
vivid reality, even as it destroys the notion that language is a transparent medium. It leaves us with a signifying surface that, because
so transgressive and astonishing, fractures our expectations of how
language represents the world. By making language theatrical—a
performance or spectacle—Barnes constructs a rift between language and experience, although this rift is not as self-conscious or
explicit as it is in the writing of Marguerite Duras. Given what
Barnes represents, in addition to the split between language and
experience she also produces a dramatic gap between culture and
its destruction, as Woolf will do (five years later) in *Between the
Acts*. Here, as in *Between the Acts*, the split between culture and
its destruction results in textual "erotics," language that moves
along the line of fault formed by such a rift.[5]

In *Ariel and the Police*, Frank Lentricchia maintains that the desire for lyricism is a contradictory impulse. On the one hand, it responds to the cartography of imperialistic structures of containment
and domination. The desire for lyricism—a "politics of lyricism"—
produces writing without plot or historical subject, writing that
does not conform to the structures of any philosophical system. On
the other hand, it satisfies desires stimulated by consumer capitalism; such writing is an "improvisational song of desire, a writing
about itself in the sense that the 'itself' is a longing as language
eking itself out, each phrase a kind of blind adventure going nowhere, an infinite and exquisite foreplay" (202). Despite the Derridean overtones of his language, Lentricchia's point is more Marxist
than deconstructionist: for Lentricchia, such writing reinscribes
"the epic of bourgeois interiority, wherein the life of the spirit is
hard to distinguish from the special sort of desire stimulated in the
time and place of first-world consumer capitalism" (204). Our longing for lyricism, from this point of view, is a longing for an escape
from the quotidian, the highly structured routines and rituals of our
lives that leave so little room for play or spontaneity. What we want

most, Lentricchia notes, is to be thrilled and captivated by such writing.

Barnes's longing to escape from history is expressed in *Nightwood* as a longing for the destruction of culture, and the language is indeed thrilling and captivating. The text provides for a reader something like the escape from the quotidian and the historical that Robin and Nora find in the theatricality of their own passion. Individual passions and pleasures take precedence over any kind of larger context or community. They and we withdraw into a space that is unusually complex, for in their relationship each plays the part of lover, mother, and daughter—and, for us as we read, other kinds of boundaries, such as those separating culture and its destruction, become blurred. Concomitant with this use of prose and retreat from society, however, is Barnes's insistence on the historical, on the concrete, undeniable, atrocious results of material conditions on subjectivities within larger cultural configurations. These are impulses Barnes links with culture as effects of culture, inseparable from it and especially from its horrors and atrocities. Therefore, the text is profoundly contradictory for the reader, who experiences the split between ahistorical impulses and historical imperatives.

When in 1932 and 1933 Barnes was writing what would eventually become *Nightwood*, she planned to call it *Bow Down: Anatomy of Night*. Her use of *Bow Down* as a working title indicates that power, embodied either in individuals or social institutions, was central to her design. To bow down is to become humble to external authority, to collapse under the weight of overwhelming, insupportable grief. Field argues that the phrase "bow down" does not imply becoming humble to external authorities but instead points to "man's descent back into the kingdom of the animal, which is something both preferable to his human captivity and yet obscene" (183). In a sense he is right: the animal world does exert an extraordinary force here as a realm uninscribed by cultural forms of power and domination. It is a region unmapped and forgotten—or better yet, repressed—by culture; it is dangerous because it cannot be articulated and thus tamed by discourse and consciousness. It is fitting that Barnes chose the chapter title "Watchman, What of the Night" from Isaiah 21, for there the oracle cries: "My heart flutters, dread makes me tremble, the twilight I longed for has become my horror" (21:4). *Nightwood* explores the horror of the twilight—

the loss of consciousness, the destruction—we long for. To descend back into the animal kingdom is to move toward a place uninscribed by history—it is prehistory brought into the present and thus made ahistoric. Because it preexists language, it cannot be known through language. It is a place unstructured by hierarchy: difference is horizontal, not vertical. Therefore there are no clear distinctions between good and evil, humans and beasts, or masculine and feminine. For all these reasons it is alluring, terrifying, and distinctly not human.

At the same time that it is ahistorical, the text records events with historical specificity. It, like Isaiah, links degradation, destruction, and bowing down to the painful survival of the Jewish community, a particular group of marginalized people. This connection is perhaps most apparent in Guido and his son Felix, although all of *Nightwood*'s figures are constantly bowing down or "going down." The effects of exclusion, subjection, and vulnerability are personally and socially devastating, as we see in the initial portraits of Guido. This evidence of pain produced by historical circumstances contradicts those aspects of the text that seem ahistorical or universal.

Nightwood begins in 1880 with the birth of Felix Volkbein, Guido's son, "in spite of a well-founded suspicion as to the advisability of perpetuating that race which has the sanction of the Lord and the disapproval of the people" (1). The narrative voice is ambivalent. What are we to make of the narrator's claim that such a suspicion is "well-founded"? Written in the 1930s during a period of increasing political fascism in which Hitler rose to power, the context for such language was anything but politically neutral. If the passage is glossed as a general negation of human life by making "that race" include all races, if it is made into a metaphorical expression of modernist despair about culture and humanity, then the specificity of the passage, its particular form of anti-Semitism, is lost. Embedded in such a reading is a naturalizing, ahistorical view of human pain and despair: it claims that social, political, and economic contexts have no place in the production of human subjectivity, happiness, or suffering. Although *Nightwood* was read in the socially and politically conscious 1930s as aesthetically apolitical and even self-indulgent in its *exclusion* of relevant social and political commentary, the ways that conflicting voices in the text articulate sexual difference and Jewishness are very much political, though contradictory and disturbing because supportive of anti-Semitic impulses. At the same time, the politics of Barnes's life and art, while highly individualistic and not always consistent, shows signs of a sensitivity to institutions or individuals taking control of others' bodies and minds.[6]

Regardless of evidence from Barnes's life that demonstrates her resistance to fascistic forms of control, it is often quite difficult to determine her attitudes toward power and violence from her writing, and not just in *Nightwood*. In *Ladies Almanack* the question gets formulated in terms of her attitude toward the female body and lesbian love, which critics read not only in divergent but diametrically opposing ways and which is of interest given Barnes's own willingness to cross a cultural taboo and love another woman. (Even here, her attitude is contradictory: Barnes would say later in her life, "I'm not a lesbian. I just loved Thelma" [Field 37].) Many readers (myself included) read the *Almanack* as a celebration of the female body and lesbian love, while others have proposed that it is instead a fierce attack on lesbianism.[7] Since the book was written for the private amusement of those very women (Natalie Barney and company) it caricatures, whom Barnes knew in Paris, the latter reading is less plausible.

But the text is playful, satiric, and perhaps ambiguous enough to support opposing interpretations: it provides an especially vivid example of how a reader's own values and perspectives work to influence the positions she or he assumes. Even among those whose readings are more or less similar, reactions to particular scenes differ for complex and subtle reasons. Susan Sniader Lanser, for instance, who also reads the text as a private celebration, admits to discomfort with the final scene, which I find much more humorous than disturbing.[8] In this scene, Evangeline Musset (who is modeled on Natalie Barney) dies and her body is burned; only her tongue survives. The women rush to the ashes with a "great Commotion, and the sound of Skirts swirled in haste . . . but Seniorita Fly-About came down upon that urn first, and beatitude played and flickered upon her Face, and from under her Skirts a slow smoke issued, though no thing burned. . . . And as the day came some hundred Women were seen bent in Prayer" (84). As Lanser notes, the "glorification of the tongue as the ultimate sexual instrument must surely have provided an antidote to the ethos of phallic supremacy and clitoral insufficiency of a newly Freudian age" (44).

Here women are reduced to their genitals, and the reduction both mirrors and becomes strangely subversive of modern patriarchal culture's fetishization of the female body. Since the women's pleasure is not heterosexual, Barnes does not simply reflect patriarchal structures, and so she makes room for a position outside those structures, a position capable of subverting the authority of masculine discourses. In *Nightwood*, Barnes comments on the sort of comic attitude she uses in both texts as a defense against vulnerability and painful exposure. The passage describes Nora: "Cynicism, laughter, the second husk into which the shucked man crawls, she seemed to know little or nothing about" (53). (And if Nora is often read as a portrayal of Djuna Barnes, at least in this area Barnes was not at all like her character. Given the dark comedy of Barnes's writing and the stories of her quick wit, guarded privacy, and distance, this second husk seems to have been something she knew well.)

When the narrative voice in *Nightwood* seems to share the perspective of fascistic ideologies, it is more disturbing than Barnes's ambivalence in *Ladies Almanack*. It is even more troubling since Barnes refused to admit any connection between politics and the text, which suggests that any inscriptions of fascistic ideologies were politically unconscious on her part. Field reports that in later years Barnes "reacted violently to suggestions that the 'decadence' of *Nightwood* had anything at all to do with the spirit of Nazism" (15). She insisted on its separation from the most significant political events of its context. It is not surprising that Barnes's refusal to grant any connection between her art and the political contexts that surrounded it deeply troubles her critics who oppose fascism. Shari Benstock notes that Barnes's claims notwithstanding, the figures who populate *Nightwood* are precisely those who would be targeted by Hitler (426). She's right; against the "superior race" that would build the new society, these groups were defined as antisocial, undesirable elements and categorized in precise groups—for example, Jews, homosexuals, and transsexuals—or simply as inferior because physically weak or mentally different, like Felix and Robin's son Guido. More precisely, however, it is Barnes's treatment of these groups in the text that unravels the fixity and authority of fascistic discourses and positions; such treatment contradicts and ultimately subverts whatever fascistic traces remain. Without disputing that *Nightwood* seems at times strangely in collusion with discourses that contain and exclude and without attempting to apologize for this tendency, I would argue that the text, despite contradictions which have not been adequately addressed in the criticism, also attempts to subvert fascism. For example, its refusal of discourses that categorize and purify is apparent in the ways it represents marginality.

Jews, like lesbians, are made marginal by the dominant culture: whatever seems damning about either is produced in relation to a different norm established by that culture. Guido suffers from his sense of Jewish marginality and his haunting memories of how Christians have persecuted his ancestors. The yellow-and-black handkerchief he carries symbolizes the ordinance of 1468 which decreed that

> with a rope about its neck, Guido's race should run in the Corso for the amusement of the Christian populace, while ladies of noble birth, sitting upon spines too refined for rest, arose from their seats, and, with the red-gowned cardinals and the *Monsignori*, applauded with that cold yet hysterical abandon of a people that is at once unjust and happy, the very Pope himself shaken down from his hold on heaven with the laughter of a man who forgoes his angels that he may recapture the beast. This memory and the handkerchief that accompanied it had wrought in Guido . . . the sum total of what is the Jew. He had walked, hot, incautious and damned, his eyelids quivering over the thick eyeballs, black with the pain of a participation that, four centuries later, made him a victim, as he felt the echo in his own throat of that cry running the *Piazza Montanara* long ago . . . the degradation by which his people had survived. (2)

Guido possesses concrete historical evidence of the persecutions Jews have been subjected to, of his own marginality. In the present, such formerly public symbols are private and isolating: they cannot be read by Guido's Christian wife, Hedvig, whose demeanor is militaristic and foreboding. His knowledge of the past separates him psychologically and emotionally from the dominant Christian world. Even though far removed from the run in the Corso, Guido can still feel "the echo in his own throat of that cry . . . the degradation." Because he internalizes his culture's definitions, he is to himself always an outsider, always on the margin. His options are curtailed by having been produced by that culture, and his choice—

perhaps a poor one—to attempt to span this impossible gap with various pretenses is alienating as well as sad and futile. If, as the narrator claims, "the saddest and most futile gesture of all [was] his pretence to a barony" (3), this is because he attempts to become absorbed into the dominant culture and complicit with his persecutors.

His attempt to fashion a new identity is not particularly successful. It forces him to pretend to be radically different—with respect to ethnicity, class, and religious origins—from what he is. In addition, Guido adopts the sign of the cross—a symbol of the very group that oppresses him—and produces various signs to support his pretense to be a Christian baron: a coat of arms, a list of Christian progenitors, even portraits of Gentiles he claims are his parents. These portraits bear a superficial physical resemblance to him but are in fact "reproductions of two intrepid and ancient actors. Guido had found them in some forgotten and dusty corner and had purchased them when he had been sure that he would need an alibi for the blood" (7). But the most profound resemblance is that he is just as much an actor as they. However paranoid Guido's purchase of the portraits as an alibi for his heritage may seem, it can hardly be considered such, given what the years following the publication of *Nightwood* would demonstrate in the most unimaginable and horrible terms.

If Guido's acquisitions are attempts to be part of the dominant culture, one of the most powerful ways Barnes subverts that culture is through a refusal of the labels and titles that reproduce an oppressive status quo. Initially, Guido is described by the narrative voice with very little compassion as "mentally deficient and emotionally excessive, an addict to death; at ten, barely as tall as a child of six, wearing spectacles, stumbling when he tried to run, with cold hands and anxious face . . . trembling with an excitement that was a precocious ecstasy" (107). Guido becomes from this point of view "deficient" because he is different. But "deficient" and "excessive" are not value-free terms: they inscribe hierarchy, not just difference. Guido can be "deficient" and "excessive" only in relation to some preconceived ideal. In this case the ideal seems to be one of mental and physical strength, competence, and control. Guido does not meet these standards, and the narrator judges harshly his failure to do so.

Felix takes a different stance: as he says to Matthew O'Connor,

Guido "is not like other children, not cruel, or savage. For this very reason he is called 'strange.' A child who is mature, in the sense that the heart is mature, is always, I have observed, called deficient" (115). Felix treats Guido kindly: he is, astonishingly enough given his hopes for a son like himself, able to put aside his wishes in an effort to accept Guido as he is and, more, as someone different from himself whom he cannot understand. So, although Felix is "startled out of himself" when Guido speaks of wanting to enter the church, Felix buys him a metal Virgin and learns more about Catholicism: he does not insist on shaping his son into an image of himself, which is precisely what one expects will happen when he tells Matthew of his desire for a son "who would feel as he felt about the 'great past'" (38). Although Guido's preoccupation with Catholicism does suggest a fascination with a continuous tradition that links the past to the present, he is not obsessed with the same kind of cultural and aristocratic past that haunts Felix. His religious tendencies connect him with his mother and thus, ironically, since Catholicism is powerful in modern European culture, with her exteriority, for his actions echo Robin's earlier—if less successful—attempts at conversion. Thus, he is displaced by his associations with both mother and father.

Curiously, Matthew appears to use language reminiscent of the narrative voice but manages to shift the way that language signifies. When he says that "with Guido, you are in the presence of the 'maladjusted,'" he quickly adds that he is not "using that word in the derogatory sense at all" (116). With such a qualification he separates himself from the narrator and the tendency to write others off by labeling them in simplistic ways. Unlike the narrator, he does not intend "maladjusted" to be understood as a clinical, confining term. Both Felix and Matthew attempt to articulate Guido's value, even though they acknowledge their inability to understand him completely and even though Felix is troubled and anxious because other people say Guido is "not sound of mind" and because he "does not grow up" (120). Matthew's response connects (in a rather wonderful way) Guido with the text's more general affirmation of the possibilities in the unknown:

> The excess of his sensibilities may preclude his mind. His sanity is an unknown room: a known room is always smaller than an unknown. If I were you . . . I would carry that boy's

mind like a bowl picked up in the dark; you do not know what's in it. He feeds on odd remnants that we have not priced; he eats a sleep that is not our sleep. There is more in sickness than the name of that sickness. In the average person is the peculiar that has been scuttled, and in the peculiar the ordinary that has been sunk; people always fear what requires watching. (120)

Through his "excessive" feelings, Guido is linked with the feminine and thought to be mentally unstable. In order to alleviate Felix's discomfort with Guido's difference, Matthew produces the wonderful image of Guido's mind as a bowl whose contents, though unknown, may be valuable nevertheless. He points out that much is not contained by the signs people use in order to make sense of the world: word and thing are not identical, and for some things we have no words at all. He warns that we must proceed cautiously and refuse to rob others of their subjectivity with clinical labels constructed in what Michel Foucault has called the discourses and disciplines of knowledge and the will to truth.[9]

In "The Discourse on Language," Foucault proposes that "in every society the production of discourse is at once controlled, selected, organised and redistributed according to a certain number of procedures, whose role is to avert its powers and its dangers, to cope with chance events, to evade its ponderous, awesome materiality" (216). For example, not every topic can be spoken of, and not everyone can speak of subjects not forbidden. As a culture we set up various procedures to qualify or authorize members of society to use specialized discourses. In this way, the "danger spots" of politics and sexuality are controlled and brought into discourse in particular ways, so that it is actually *in discourse* that they exercise their power. For Foucault, discourse is not just the "verbalisation of conflicts and systems of domination, but . . . the very object of man's conflicts" (216).

There are serious problems, however, with imagining discourse more material than actual social conditions. To emphasize the power of language to the exclusion of material social conditions or, worse, to equate language with those conditions and suppose that a change in language will improve oppressive social conditions are finally conservative gestures. As Hal Foster insists, however seduced we may be by "ideas of historical ruptures and epistemological breaks, cultural forms and economic modes do not simply *die*,

and the apocalypticism of the present is finally complicit with a repressive status quo" (*Recodings* 1). *Nightwood* breaks with the conventional language and subjects of fiction, but as I've noted previously, it doesn't follow that Barnes was an activist. And as Benstock
states, the living and writing patterns not only of Barnes but of
other women writers such as Jean Rhys and Anaïs Nin reveal "complex reactions *against* the call to social and political involvement in
the period. In a political climate that demanded social relevance in
literature, these women writers . . . seem to exploit an entirely private, even secret, female experience" (424). Similarly, to make discourse the "very object of man's conflicts" can be a way to retreat
from social exigencies.

Yet discourse has some material effects, and it can be a site of
resistance. Foucault also maintains that the West uses discourse as
a vehicle for power in the form of a will to truth. The use of labels
and the containment of subjectivities are two manifestations of this
will to truth. Barnes refuses to let the language of *Nightwood* serve
as a vehicle for power: labels are suspect and subjectivities exceed
categorization and purification (which provides, perhaps, some indication why she refused to use the term "lesbian" to describe herself). Similarly, Matthew disrupts and subverts the use of such a
discourse for the workings of disciplinary power: his credentials are
suspect; he refuses to sustain the illusion of a transparent relationship between word and thing.

But Matthew's sensitivity is not mirrored by the world at large
(figured to a great extent by the narrative voice itself), and so his
words seem, according to that more conventional world and its attitudes, misguided. In his attempts to find a language capable of
providing comfort and solace in a painful world, he does not care
how hyperbolic he becomes in the process or even if he lies. Truth
is not his intent, and he questions its relevance to a more humane
and human-centered discourse. From normative perspectives, the
"remedies" he offers come at the price of "true" knowledge. But
from another, Matthew's discourse is antithetical to a fascist rhetoric that would crush difference and territorialize whatever threatens its control, whether explicitly or implicitly through the power of
the unknown.

Matthew embraces the indeterminacy of the unknown. When he
walks out on Nora, he encounters an expriest who wants to know

"whether you were ever *really* married or not" (159). Matthew refuses the terms of the question:

> Should I know that? . . . I've *said* I was married and I gave the girl a name and had children by her, then, presto! I killed her off as lightly as the death of swans. And I was reproached for that story! I was. Because even your friends regret weeping for a myth, as if that were not practically the fate of all the tears in the world! What if the girl *was* the wife of my brother and the children my brother's children? . . . Who says she might not have been mine, and the children also? Who for that matter . . . says they are not mine? (159–160)

It is hard to tell whether the woman Matthew claimed he married and loved is really the wife of his brother or whether that is yet another fiction built upon a fiction. The expriest pressures Matthew to be definitive about fact and fiction because he wants to know, once and for all, "what is what." For Matthew, that kind of truth is irrelevant if not impossible to know conclusively. He implies that those we grieve for are products of our own fantasies and idealizations rather than "real" subjects as they might exist apart from our imaginings. Most of the weeping in the world is, therefore, just for one myth or another. Ultimately it makes no difference what is real and what is fantasy—at least with respect to human suffering and pain. To care too much about what is fact and what is fiction is to be "right down in the mud without a feather to fly with" (160).

If categories such as "the maladjusted" are attempts to fix identity in ways that not only can be articulated but also organized according to principles of exclusion and thus known and controlled, then Matthew's attempt to change how we use such terms mirrors the text's larger project of questioning human knowledge by propelling what we think we know into the unknown. It undermines individuals' efforts to produce, fix, and define identity with titles. When figures in the text use such categories or titles, their efforts to make sense or give shape express what they intend inadequately. Their efforts simultaneously suggest their desire to be what they are not, to be persons of social significance and power, and make them as well as their so-called legitimate counterparts in mainstream culture seem ludicrous. These counterparts, such as the Count, are exposed as just as dependent upon arbitrary constructs as are their "debased" reflections. Neither the powerful nor the powerless are immune to Barnes's critique.

Like his father, Felix calls himself Baron, but his attempt to attach himself with words to the aristocracy merely makes his exclusion from it more radical and absolute. The title provides no real clue to his identity but instead obscures it, putting more distance between word and thing, making his public self inauthentic. The imagined private self that would by contrast be authentic is so radically inaccessible as to be beyond articulation and knowledge, to be virtually nonexistent. Some, like Felix, attempt to redefine and thus subvert the categories into which they fall, but if Felix can hide his Jewishness and Matthew can hide his transvestism, others cannot hide and are persecuted simply because they are different or disabled. The weak are especially vulnerable, as we see most painfully when Matthew tells the story of Mademoiselle Basquette, a girl without legs who wheeled herself through the Pyrenees on a board. Her difference and disability are constantly apparent, and because her vulnerability is so visible she is prey to the likes of the sailor who rapes her and then puts her back on her board miles away from town.

Titles promise an escape from identity and vulnerability because they construct an artificial self for the subject, a wall between the person and the world. Significant human contact or community among the circus people is minimal, but Felix feels most at home with these people who have adopted estranging titles similar to his own. Like him, they have "seized on titles for a purpose. . . . They [take] titles merely to dazzle boys about town, to make their public life (and it was all they had) mysterious and perplexing" (11). Titles work to distance individuals from each other and from themselves and make them feel less vulnerable. When Felix clings to his title to "dazzle his own estrangement" (11), he makes a spectacle of his lack of identity.

Like Felix, Frau Mann takes a title (the Duchess of Broadback) to mask her lack of identity and produces an image or spectacle of herself instead. Her desire to see the living statues and the Count is an ironic comment on her own objectification and estrangement, for she fails to recognize the extent to which she is like them. Frau Mann describes the Count as "*something* that must be seen" (13, emphasis mine). Her discourse objectifies him, unconsciously reflecting the way she herself has been objectified and perpetuating oppressive structures. To look at objectified others is, for her, to gaze into a mirror:

> In her face was the tense expression of an organism surviving in an alien element. She seemed to have a skin that was the pattern of her costume: a bodice of lozenges, red and yellow . . . red tights, laced boots—one somehow felt they ran through her as the design runs through hard holiday candies, and the bulge in the groin where she took the bar, one foot caught in the flex of the calf, was as solid, specialized, and as polished as oak. The stuff of her tights was no longer a covering, it was herself; the span of the tightly stitched crotch was so much her own flesh that she was as unsexed as a doll. The needle that had made one the property of the child made the other the property of no man. (13)

Felix is intrigued by the notion that Frau Mann could have at one time been involved with the Count because she seems so utterly asexual. And she seems asexual because she has become dehumanized, identical with her work. Her trapeze costume *is* her skin; it runs through her tissue like the design that continues on the inside of hard candies; her crotch is covered over and sealed. Although "the property of no man," Frau Mann is still objectified, a commodity. It's her defining characteristic. Sewn into a form as rigid as a doll, there's no life, no desire, left. She escapes being contained and controlled as the property of some man, but subjection, Barnes suggests, is more complex than this.

Titles and labels signify not only the circumscription and control of consciousness but of the body as well. Perhaps to a greater extent than any other woman of her time, Barnes was able to write the body into language, and she did so in ways that expose and critique inscriptions of power on human subjects. Foucault links such an inscription of power to the development of capitalism. In order to analyze the signifying power of the body, *Discipline and Punish* traces transformations in the ways criminals have been treated in the West. Under the monarchies that preceded capitalism, punishment was directed against the offender's body in public, theatrical rites of torture orchestrated by the sovereign—all offenses were understood to be offenses against the sovereign. With the increasingly important status of property, the emerging capitalist state required new forms of punishment and control. At this time, Foucault argues, the implementation of social control shifted from directly controlling bodies through pain to controlling bodies through their minds with representations (such as the idea of pain and the mental torture produced by such an idea). In this appropriation of minds, the mind is inscribed upon as if it were a tablet. The shift occurred because modern capitalist society requires subjects who will respect not the authority of the sovereign but the authority of property. It requires subjects who will police themselves and who will, seemingly of their own accord, choose subjection.

In *Nightwood*, the effects of power on the body and consciousness are circular, for while one form of power controls the body through the inscription of consciousness, another controls consciousness by writing on the body. This interrelationship is apparent in Matthew's use of the black body to signify sexuality and depravity: he describes Nikka, who "used to fight the bear in the Cirque de Paris" crouched naked except for an "ill-concealed loincloth all abulge as if with a deep-sea catch, tattooed from head to heel with all the *ameublement* of depravity" (16). Written on Nikka's body are words and images of Western culture, a culture not his own but which has nonetheless inscribed his body and structured his mind: he is willing to fight the beast for the pleasure of white European audiences. By gazing at the spectacle of Nikka and the beast, such audiences can distance themselves from nonhuman qualities they project onto Nikka, from aspects of their own sexuality and their capacity for depravity. In their racism they are like the pope and the so-called refined Christian populace who witnessed the run in the Corso that haunts Guido's memory and significantly informs his understanding of what it means to be a Jew. Both instances are examples of how the irrational and demonic components of the unconscious are given legitimate, if horrible and indefensible, cultural expression.

That Nikka's body is literally inscribed emphasizes his subjection to white male culture and separates Barnes's portrayal from Matthew's. For she comments, however indirectly, on his signifying power and undermines it as natural or given by exposing it as culturally determined, whereas Matthew's discourse fails to suggest any such awareness. Although Nikka is made to signify sexuality, the writing on his body robs him of his own capacity for sexual pleasure. What he signifies is not equivalent to the fact of his situation. Matthew claims that despite this representation of virility, Nikka himself is impotent: "He couldn't have done a thing (and I

know what I am talking about in spite of all that has been said about
the black boys) . . . though (it's said) at a stretch it spelled Desde-
mona" (16). Matthew's discourse ("black boys") is racist. "Desde-
mona" suggests miscegenation and violence: what makes Nikka
impotent may in fact be that his penis has been tattooed. That it is
tattooed with a word that can only be read "at a stretch" (when
erect) makes the word into an implicit warning and Nikka's impo-
tence a form of punishment, a sign of the violence white male culture can inflict on the black man if he desires a white woman. In
this way Nikka is dehumanized in order that he may produce cultural significance. He is like the living statues that Felix and Frau
Mann come to see at Count Onatorio Altamonte's. Moreover, he
consents to this use of his body: he performs willingly.

But by having Matthew use such language, Barnes runs the risk
of seeming to adopt Matthew's dehumanizing stance herself. This
portrayal produces an extraordinarily difficult and complex dilemma. The dilemma is similar to issues related to radical forms of
performance art or film, which raise questions about whether the
female (black) body can be used to deconstruct sexist (racist) representations or whether the mere fact of using the body perpetuates
sexism (racism). Denaturalizing what seems natural or given is to
intervene in the ideological work that such images perform in cultural contexts. And as Hal Foster notes, complicity is necessarily a
part of any deconstructive enterprise. In a discussion of feminist art
involved with Lacanian psychoanalysis, Foster argues that "if this
work elicits our desire for an image of woman, truth, certainty, clo-
sure, it does so only to draw it out from its traditional captures (e.g.
voyeurism, narcissism, scopophilia, fetishism), to reflect back the
(masculine) gaze to the point of self-consciousness" (*Recodings* 8).
A similar principle is at work in Barnes's portrayal of Matthew portraying Nikka. And yet this principle remains disturbing because it
is in collusion with what it seeks to disrupt. It makes readers and
viewers confront their own complicity and contradictory responses.

Barnes's treatment of male sexuality subverts conventional notions of masculinity, male power, and authority—and typical female
responses to these notions. Those who at least initially seem more
viril, Nikka and the Count, are impotent whereas Felix is "not sufficient to make [Robin] what he had hoped" (44). At the top of
Nightwood's social hierarchy, and thus its most socially and politically powerful figure, Count Onatorio Altamonte is titled, wealthy,
white, heterosexual, and male. Felix's first encounter with a "gen-

tleman of quality" is with the Count (12). But, although he hasn't given up the idea of sexual desire, the Count fears that he will become impotent. When he returns to the crowded house with a young girl in a riding habit, he immediately throws them all out. Matthew explains that it is "for one of those hopes that is about to be defeated. . . . Count Onatorio Altamonte . . . suspected he had come upon his last erection" (25). If this hope is "about to be defeated," the Count is already impotent.

In the most explicit rejection of masculinity and male sexuality, a rejection at once comic and poignant, the text's central male figure, Matthew O'Connor, takes out his penis and speaks to it, subjecting it to humiliation:

> I spoke to Tiny O'Toole because it was his turn; I had tried
> everything else. There was nothing for it this time but to make
> him face the mystery so it could see him clear as it saw me.
> So then I whispered, "What is this thing, Lord?" And I began
> to cry; the tears went like rain goes down on the world without
> touching the face of Heaven. Suddenly I realized that it was
> the first time in my life my tears were strange to me because
> they went straight forward out of my eyes; I was crying because
> I had to embarrass Tiny like that for the good it might do
> him. (132)

Given the phallocratic culture of the West, such an undoing of the sign of male power and privilege is rather delightful and liberating. At the same time, Matthew's pain is awful and heart wrenching.

The text's representation of differences in sexuality is its most effective undermining of oppressive cultural structures and of its tendency to seem strangely in collusion with such structures. The text's vanishing point is its undoing of institutionalized heterosexuality: it insists not only on Matthew's difference as a transvestite but on the difference of lesbian passion and love. In both cases the clinical labels attached to difference are subverted. And in both the feminine is privileged—heterosexuality is refused. It is when Robin's thoughts have wandered to other women that Felix finds her asleep after reading the memoirs of the Marquis de Sade. Initially a sign of indifference or boredom, her sleep turns to fear when she awakens to find Felix. She rejects his attempts to comfort her and pushes him away. It is as if her encounter with masculine rituals of sadistic sexuality and violence influences, perhaps even in part causes, her rejection of heterosexual marriage (something she seems to have drifted into more than chosen). Robin's initial indifference and subsequent fear make an important point: one cannot merely ignore oppressive structures or imagine them away. Robin's reasons for fear are justified. Even if Barnes's text subverts the dominant culture's phallocentric bias, other cultural texts (including Sade) do not, and, more important, a subversive text cannot in itself alter its cultural context (though it may contribute to such a project). *Nightwood*'s difference from that cultural context works most effectively against the traces of collusion with oppressive forces that riddle the text.

Like Guido, Robin is outside mainstream culture; even more, she is, like the beggar woman in Duras's *The Vice Consul*, antithetical to culture itself. An enigma more unreal than human, she is projected on the screen of the others' desires. Like Caddy Compson in Faulkner's *The Sound and the Fury*, she has no voice and functions as the object of others' desires: they create her. Unlike Caddy, however, Robin is not constructed as the product of masculine imaginings and projections, for, apart from her early marriage to Felix, she is desired by women or explained by a man who experiences himself as a woman. Although Robin's difference in sexuality propels Barnes's representations into an alternative textual space, at the same time Nora's and Jenny's possessive forms of love are not all that different from heterosexual forms.

Robin's difference from any human norm is established immediately through her connections with nature—with plants and animals—and her radical separation from what is enduring and traditional is established by her inability to convert to Catholicism, perhaps even to take it seriously. She prays in church, unable to "offer herself up," unable to be anything but what she is, unable, too, to be anything but miserable. She is troubled by her "preoccupation that was its own predicament" (47). The exact nature of the preoccupation is never elaborated, which gives it the effect of being all the more powerful, like Robin herself, because so mysterious and undefined. Yet, in the midst of her misery, out of "some hidden capacity, some lost subterranean humour," when bowing down in church she laughs (47). Barnes does not attempt to explicate this hidden capacity for laughter, which is unmapped by consciousness or volition. But as Hélène Cixous suggests, women's capacity for laughter is a disrupting and disturbing force; it can be a refusal of patriarchal institutions such as the church, a refusal to march in line.[10] Although Barnes is not as utopian as Cixous, whose work is most valuable for its capacity to inspire rather than for its ability to be put to pragmatic uses, Robin's difference is underscored by her laughter, which shatters the silence of the church. Laughter may be dangerous and subversive but if it liberates her at all, it does so only in passing, for at the next moment she is sleepwalking once again.

As figures who subvert conventional gender roles, Robin Vote and Matthew O'Connor are not simply feminine and masculine respectively but are instead the "third sex." Robin, the "tall girl with the body of a boy," produces an androgynous image in her white flannel trousers and lacquered pumps. Biologically male, Matthew is "the last woman left in this world . . . the bearded lady" (100), "the other woman that God forgot" (143). Strangely enough, although literally bearded he is also more conventionally feminine, more defined by patriarchal discourses—which he internalizes in order to shape his femininity—than any biological female in the text. Unlike the women, his desires are shaped by what it has traditionally meant to be a woman: "No matter what I may be doing, in my heart is the wish for children and knitting. God, I never asked better than to boil some good man's potatoes and toss up a child for him every nine months" (91). No woman in the text has such desires—they do not knit, take care of men, or produce children. There is no Mrs. Dalloway or Mrs. Ramsey in Barnes's textual world. To some extent, then, Matthew's forms of femininity actually reconstruct cultural definitions of gender rather than subvert them.

To undo gender as it is constructed by culture is to move toward what culture represses. In this respect *Nightwood* echoes the Night Town of Joyce's *Ulysses* but with a twist, substituting in its title the natural image of wood for the cultural image of the town. The title suggests Joyce but points toward the differences between Barnes's and Joyce's treatment of the irrational and surreal, taboo desires, and what is so repressed by society that it can be approached only in the night, if indeed psychic structures will allow it to be experienced at all. For both, cross-dressing and gender inversions figure the absence of rationality and cultural order, as Sandra Gilbert and Susan Gubar have noted, though the significance of that absence is different in each.[11] Barnes and Joyce see the maintenance of dichotomized gender difference as essential to social order; in *Nightwood*, clothing articulates the limitations of equating gender with biological sex as part of a more general critique of "dressing the unknowable in the garments of the known." As representatives of the third sex, Robin and Matthew are more than simply feminine and masculine members of a particular social order. There is something *right* about the third sex, which, like the doll, is "sacred *and* profane" (142, emphasis mine).

In a review of Brenda Maddox's *Nora: The Real Life of Molly Bloom*, Carolyn Heilbrun writes that although Leopold Bloom is androgynous, "it is arguable whether or not Joyce could have allowed any woman, in or out of literature, to be so" (5). In Night Town, the inversion of masculine and feminine roles is not sacred and profane, it is simply profane. There is nothing sacred about Bella transforming into Bello, and Bloom's transformation into a woman signifies his maladjustment and the dangers of pushing androgyny too far. It thus plays into male fears of becoming too feminine and is instructive about what will happen as a result. As a woman, Bloom is exposed to a public spectacle of degradation, pain, and humiliation that eventually restores the rational, as symbolized by the male's assertion of his masculine sexual "rights" and priorities. The sadomasochistic ritual is Bloom's punishment for succumbing to what Bella, or Bello, calls "petticoat government" and for being dangerously "feminine" himself. It is a punishment and degradation that he (or his feminine self) desires.

Bloom's "femininity" is linked to a masochistic desire to be controlled, in both mind and body. He assumes femininity as a role; he plays out a fantasy that is but a part of who he is and that is radically different from his ordinary appearance in society. Bello responds in the anticipated and predictable sadistic manner demanded by the dichotomous structure Joyce puts into operation. Bello promises to make Bloom like one of his whores, a process that he will control by transforming Bloom's body: "As they are now, so will you be, wigged, singed, perfumesprayed, ricepowdered, with smoothshaven armpits. Tape measurements will be taken next your skin. You will be laced with cruel force into vicelike corsets of soft dove coutille, with whalebone busk, to the diamond trimmed pelvis . . . while your figure, plumper than when at large, will be restrained in nettight frocks" (535). As the female Bella becomes the male Bello, what emerges is a parodic expression of how modern patriarchal culture imagines, despises, and fears the female who assumes the male position of privilege and power. Bello puts his

heel on Bloom's neck and commands: "Feel my entire weight. Bow,
bond-slave, before the throne of your despot's glorious heels, so glis-
tening in their proud erectness" (531). In this episode Joyce asserts
that in males feminine characteristics are twisted and skewed, as
are masculine characteristics in females. Unlike *Nightwood*, the
bowing down in Night Town is sadomasochistic; it is exclusively
to the power embodied in an individual who is able to exercise that
power over others' minds and bodies. The significance of bowing
down is therefore much more limited and less heterogeneous than
in *Nightwood*, where bowing down simultaneously signifies a number of contradictory actions, from bowing down to cultural authority
to bowing down before the more overwhelming magnitude of the
indeterminable to bowing down from the weight of insupportable
grief.

Although the Night Town episode is surrealistic, it partakes of
and remains within culturally constructed gender hierarchies. To
be feminine here is to be degraded because women's minds and
bodies are restricted and dominated by men. While in this presen-
tation there is an implicit critique of such domination, Joyce does
not explore the subversive potential of the victim or outsider: he
instead explores the territorialization of those others, including the
production of their own taboo desires. It is taboo for a man to express, as Bloom does, submissive, demeaning, degrading qualities
that the culture defines as feminine. In this culture, as John Berger's analysis of Western art has shown, we are only comfortable
when women express such qualities.[12]

Such degradation is very different from what we find in *Nightwood*. When Matthew dons women's gowns, it is not to engage in
sadomasochistic, ritualized behaviors. In fact, as Nora describes it,
the image becomes one of considerable power and strength: "Is not
the gown the natural raiment of extremity? What nation, what religion, what ghost, what dream, has not worn it—infants, angels,
priests, the dead; why should not the doctor, in the grave dilemma
of his alchemy, wear his dress?" (80) If the gown empowers Matthew by giving public form to what he experiences as a private and
unconventional reality, Bloom's temporary movement toward his
own repressed desires and fantasies—irrational from the perspective of the dominant culture—empowers him in a very different,
more conventional way. For it is after the Night Town episode
that Bloom is able to restore heterosexual order by returning to a
more assertive, conventionally masculine position: he is able to

reassert himself sexually with Molly and resume their disrupted sexual relations.

As radical as its representations of differences in sexuality are, however, Barnes's text finally fails to escape oppressive cultural structures because of the ways such structures have always already influenced consciousness. For instance, by "wandering away" from heterosexuality, Robin does not simply walk into a lesbian utopia: her relationships with women are marked by violence, pain, and possessiveness. Her difference in sexual orientation is not liberating: it is women, not men, who seek to control her. By hopping from bed to bed she refuses to be possessed but leads a tortured life that precludes real intimacy.

One of the reasons for the failure of lesbian love to achieve a desirable alternative to heterosexuality in the text is that these women have internalized the violence toward and hatred of women in Western culture. Matthew describes the curses he's heard women scream at one another in the public toilets at night. Their anger is violent, and it is marked by self-loathing: "May you be damned to hell! May you die standing upright! May you be damned upward! May this be damned, terrible and damned spot! May it wither into the grin of the dead, may this draw back, low riding mouth in an empty snarl of the groin! May this be your torment, may this be your damnation!" (95). By damning the clitoris these women damn their own sexual pleasure as well as that of other women. They have been inscribed by the violence of Western society in ways that structure subjectivity and desire.

Nora's and Jenny's attempts to possess and dominate Robin are marked by violence that is especially acute when they are insecure about the extent or effectiveness of their control. They mimic the worst kinds of aggressive masculine behavior. After a desperate attempt to manipulate Robin during the carriage ride with Matthew, the English girl, and the child, Jenny proclaims that while men know nothing about love, women "should know—they are finer, more sacred; my love is sacred and my love is great" (75). Robin rejects this position of sameness and superiority simply due to gender and tells Jenny to shut up, that she doesn't know what she's talking about. Jenny embraces sexual difference in loving Robin but not Robin's difference from herself (or, more accurately, Jenny's idealized version of herself). In a desperate attempt to deny and control this latter difference, Jenny attacks, scratching and hitting Robin with a violence that the child, who watches the entire spectacle, finds intolerable.

It is from women, not men, that Robin receives her blows. Though she shies away from Felix after reading Sade, when she is struck by women it is as if she has no strength or will with which to protect herself. When Nora fears she cannot possess Robin, that "it is over," she strikes Robin as she sleeps, forcibly waking her. The horrible reality of her action torments Nora: "I saw her come awake and turn befouled before me, she who had managed in that sleep to keep whole. . . . I didn't know, I didn't know it was to be me who was to do the terrible thing! No rot had touched her until then, and there before my eyes I saw her corrupt all at once" (145). The change seems to occur entirely within Nora. She first idealizes Robin and then in her anger imagines that she has the power to make Robin corrupt. Robin, however, is not pure or immune to violent impulses. Felix sees her holding their child Guido as if she were to dash him down to the floor. Nora finds her holding the doll that is their symbolic child in an identical posture. Although Robin brings her son down gently, she will later smash the doll, an act that challenges, symbolically, the way culture constructs the mother as unambivalently loving, devoted, and self-sacrificing.

Despite her rejection of motherhood and her attempt to destroy the symbol of the child she cannot have with Nora, Robin herself is frequently associated with childhood. Therefore, it seems fitting that she speaks most loquaciously with the child at Jenny's party and then later with a young English woman, for it is as if her more natural and comfortable connections are with the very young. Nora's belief that Robin was somehow unsullied and innocent until she, Nora, struck her awake reinforces this image. Similarly, Nora notices how childlike Matthew seems when she visits him in the night. She again casts herself as more experienced and knowing, even though she goes to him (at least at first) for what she thinks he can teach her. "You're so like a child," she says to Matthew (133); in reference to Robin she remarks, "I saw her always like a tall child who had grown up the length of the infant's gown, walking and needing help and safety" (145).

But Matthew is skeptical about childhood as a time of innocence, free from pain and cultural conditioning. And he reminds Nora that she herself knows better: "You know as well as I do that we were born twelve, and brought up thirteen, and that some of us lived" (152). Matthew asserts that childhood is an adult fantasy, that as a time of innocence and freedom it is largely imaginary. External pressures and cultural shaping are already at work. Still, childlike qualities reveal aspects of the self that have not been completely territorialized and produced by the dominant culture. To be child-like is to be toward the "other side" of how one will eventually be positioned and will position oneself according to the various categories of race, gender, and class.

Nora's dreams map the early conflict between unconscious desires and cultural taboos that in part produce contradictory impulses and show that such conflict and contradiction continue, assuming different forms in one's psychic life. Nora's dreams figure what desires remain too taboo to acknowledge; they also eclipse the emotional importance of the mother and suggest that the contradictory impulses of love and hate coexist. The first dream brings out the emotional importance of other women in her life, and re-creates the original moment of traumatic loss, the separation from her mother. It is a dream she has dreamt before but never before dreamt well. As if the original moment of separation from her mother were too painful even for a dream, her grandmother stands in for her absent mother. Nora confides that in her childhood she loved her grandmother more than anyone, but even if her relationship with her grandmother is so close, it does not account for the complete absence of her mother. After Nora's second dream Matthew notes her mother's absence and, projecting himself into her situation, responds with the cry, "It's my mother without argument I want" (149).

In the first dream, Nora is standing in a room that both seems and does not seem to be her grandmother's. Although her grandmother's belongings—portraits of her husband and writing instruments—are in the room, it nevertheless has the feel of the "nest of a bird which will not return" (62). Nora is left behind. Nora's desire to recover the lost closeness with her grandmother is an impossible desire: the complete connection she longs for with the woman she loved most cannot be realized, as her grandmother's absence—as well as her mother's—from the dream suggests. Robin takes the grandmother's place: it is the entry of Robin that makes it a dream that Nora knows she is dreaming for the last time. Yet, despite Robin's presence, she remains as inaccessible as the absent grandmother. Nora wants Robin to come into the room with her, "knowing it was impossible because the room was taboo. The louder she cried the farther away went the floor below, as if Robin and she, in their extremity, were a pair of opera glasses turned to the wrong end, diminishing in their painful love" (62).

Without this other, Nora fears she will cease to exist. Her grandmother is absent from the room Nora has constructed, and in this room Nora doubts her own existence. She longs to "put her hands on something in this room to prove it; [but] the dream had never permitted her to do so" (63). Nora does not specify what she wants to put her hands on, but if, as Jane Marcus maintains, she wants to touch the plume and inkwell, the dream points toward a belief that it is through language that she can produce a self.[13] At the same time, though, she recognizes that this enterprise involves doing something to Robin and to her grandmother, making them both "disfigured and eternalized by the hieroglyphics of sleep and pain" (63). To write is to disfigure and to eternalize, as Robin is disfigured and eternalized by the dreams and by Nora's conscious representations.

In the dream, triangles form between Robin, the grandmother, and Nora, but the identity of each merges with the others in a series of shifting and disfiguring substitutions. Nora seems indistinguishable from the grandmother in drag because it is Nora who orchestrates the dream and symbolizes Robin, who does something to her; Robin thus becomes like the child Nora, seduced by the grandmother; Robin and the grandmother are figured as cross-dressers and as women who are continually in the process of leaving the space that Nora has constructed for them. Nora's construction of a room that is not really her grandmother's mirrors what she does in constructing a space for Robin in which Robin cannot live. Thus it is hardly surprising that Robin is rarely there, even though they arrange their physical space together, for the psychic architecture that fits Nora simply doesn't work with her grandmother or Robin, no matter how close her bond with either one of them.

Nora's love is both homoerotic and incestuous: Robin—the forbidden whom she can't understand and who thus has the power to produce terror—is to Nora at once lover, mother, and child. Unable to admit the incestuous element in her love or determined to forget it, Nora represses it from consciousness but dreams it in the form of her grandmother. It is fitting that Robin, the new love, enters into this dream, making it "complete" even in its fragmented and disjointed quality, its series of substitutions.

The dream leads not to another dream but rather to a childhood memory of the grandmother encountered in a corner of the house, pointing to the basis of dreams in the material conditions and contexts of individual lives and the dreamlike quality of memory. Nora is not only abandoned, she is betrayed. Dressed as a man, Nora's grandmother approaches her with a "leer of love [and says] 'My little sweetheart' " (63). Two forbidden loves converge, one homosexual, the other incestuous. Her beloved grandmother, "for some unknown reason" in tight trousers and red waistcoat, suddenly betrays her by seeming unfamiliar, strange, and theatrical. That this image of her grandmother as a circus performer should appear to her after this particular dream suggests a symbolic connection between the events of the dream and memory. In addition, the image incorporates the love of Nora's adult life: a woman who dresses as a man, a woman she meets at the circus (hence her grandmother's outlandish outfit), and a woman whose love she cannot absolutely count on (like her grandmother who frightens her with a leer, awakens her sexually, and then betrays her by dying).

The image of the grandmother is, in addition, extraordinarily significant in the context of Barnes's own life. As Mary Lynn Broe notes in "My Art Belongs to Daddy," Barnes's relationship with her own grandmother, Zadel Barnes, was extremely complex. Broe examines letters Zadel sent to Djuna—letters that are explicitly erotic—and argues that Zadel seems to have both protected Djuna from her father (in the sense that she offered her an alternative, female-centered world) and violated her (by denying her "access to knowledge, to power, and her own voice. . . . At work is a seduction into family fantasies. . . . Boundaries are transgressed; the duty to protect and the right to use get irrevocably confused" [48]). If in Woolf's *Between the Acts* incest is shaped to a great extent through allusion, in *Nightwood*'s dream scene Barnes more explicitly portrays a relationship with incestuous overtones. And she represents her experience of it as essentially ambivalent and contradictory. The grandmother is loved and hated, desired and feared. Barnes offers an experience of love that cannot be understood within existing cultural discourses on family structures and relationships but one that makes emotional sense within this particular family. For Woolf and Barnes, the dynamics of incest are represented in language that struggles against itself. While their language works to reveal an experience unshaped by existing "official" discourses, it simultaneously struggles to conceal what is transgressive and shameful.

When Nora awakens from the first dream, she must face the re-

ality of Robin's betrayal. She looks out the window into the garden,
where she is unable to distinguish Robin and Jenny, who are locked
together in an embrace, from the lines and shadows of the statue
of the "tall granite woman bending forward with lifted head" (55).
In the ensuing moments of extremity, standing motionless like a
statue herself, Nora peers into the "faint light of dawn" until her
eyes meet Robin's and they stare at one another—each as if the
other were a living statue. By bringing her lover into the garden
outside Nora's window, Robin stages a spectacle for Nora's gaze—a
spectacle that will make Nora a child whose trust is finally completely shattered. The horrifying and incontrovertible fact of Robin's
betrayal seems not only quite literally evil but of sufficient magnitude to destroy Nora. She imagines that the force of her emotions
will change this awful reality, that "the design would break and melt
back into Robin alone" (64). Needless to say, though, her wishing
for it does not make it so, and shortly thereafter Robin sails with
Jenny for America.

After Robin leaves, Nora has to admit that the material and psychic spaces she has constructed for Robin don't work. She therefore
seeks Robin on Robin's own ground, in the night at cafes, in Mar-
seilles, Tangier, and Naples. It is when she sees a young girl who
strikes a pose similar to Robin's, of half sleeping and half suffering,
that she realizes what she has been to Robin: "Looking from her to
the Madonna behind the candles, I knew that the image, to her,
was what I had been to Robin, not a saint at all, but a fixed dismay,
the space between the human and the holy head, the arena of the
'indecent' eternal. At that moment I stood in the centre of eroticism
and death" (157–158). By getting outside herself and seeing herself
from Robin's point of view, as a "fixed dismay" or a contradictory
subject, Nora begins the painful process of deidealization. She sees
herself not as pure, spiritual, and disembodied but in the split between body and spirit. She describes the place of this realization as
the "centre of eroticism and death." It is a place where desire connects not only with the annihilation of the ego and individuality but
with the desire to destroy the other, the beloved. Robin flees from
death, as Matthew suggests, by engaging in a succession of encounters to escape the kind of serious attachment that would force
her to be aware of the inevitability of death and the hostilities that
coexist with love.

Nora's second dream explicitly links eroticism and death and provides another way of understanding the seriousness and the terror of her involvement with Robin. In Nora's second dream her grandmother is dead, her father living, and she herself a figure in the dream who is asleep and unable to act. But the dreaming self observes what the dreamed self does not. This is a powerful image, for it suggests a nascent awareness of herself as unseeing and the beginning of a new understanding of that unaware self. What the Nora who sleeps in the dream cannot see the dreaming Nora does:

> There in my sleep was my grandmother, whom I loved more than anyone, tangled in the grave grass, and flowers blowing about and between her; lying there in the grave, in the forest, in a coffin of glass, and flying low, my father who is still living; low going and into the grave beside her, his head thrown back and his curls lying out, struggling with her death terribly, and me, stepping about its edges, walking and wailing without a sound; round and round, seeing them struggling with that death as if they were struggling with the sea and my life; I was weeping and unable to do anything or take myself out of it. . . . It went on forever, though it had stopped, my father stopped beating and just lay there floating beside her, immovable, yet drifting in a tight place. And I woke up and still it was going on; it went down into the dark earth of my waking as if I were burying them with the earth of my lost sleep. (149)

There is an unusual intimacy in this dream between Nora's father and grandmother. Together they are visible to the world, especially to Nora, and yet insulated from it. Nora is unable to make her presence known to them, and when she awakes she wants to repress or bury the image of her father drifting in that tight place with his mother. Moreover, Nora recognizes his rage as something that *she* has done to her grandmother (after all, it is her dream), dreaming through her father. And it is something she has done to Robin as well. The violent impulse is her own, though she fears and disowns it by projecting it onto her father. Within the context of what we know of the Barnes family's particular erotic arrangements, it is perhaps also indicative of Barnes's rage at both her father and grandmother, as well as her recognition of the complexities of the relationship between her father and his mother.

Nora's love for Robin becomes a figurative act of murder, which is something that Nora recognizes only gradually and with great difficulty. As soon as Robin is loved and inscribed on Nora's heart, Nora "kills her" in order to possess her and preclude change. Robin ceases to exist, except ideally: "In Nora's heart lay the fossil of Robin, intaglio of her identity, and about it for its maintenance ran Nora's blood. Thus the body of Robin could never be unloved, corrupt or put away. Robin was now beyond timely changes, except in the blood that animated her" (56). The blood that animates Robin is Nora's, not her own. Thus, although Nora thinks she wants greater intimacy with Robin, her way of loving actually imposes an unbridgeable distance between them. This inscription of Robin is both beyond change and unreal, and as such it denies the constantly moving contours of what we call identity.

It is, as Nora's dreams demonstrate, in the night world that one most directly encounters the instability and contradictions of identity. Nora's refusal to admit Robin's difference despite and within the similarity of their female bodies speaks to a desire to confirm her own identity through an external love object of the same gender. It is a confirmation of their difference as a couple from the rest of the world. When Nora says, "She is myself. What am I to do?" (127) she means to suggest what she elaborates only later, that for a woman to love another woman is to break with institutionalized heterosexuality and the cultural narratives that produce it: "There's nothing to go by. . . . You do not know which way to go. A man is another person—a woman is yourself, caught as you turn in panic, on her mouth you kiss your own. If she is taken you cry that you have been robbed of yourself" (143). But Nora's language imitates the language of heterosexuality, itself an attempt to articulate similarity despite difference within the heterosexual tradition of romantic love, even while she tries to articulate her and Robin's separation from all that. As in *Wuthering Heights* when Catherine Earnshaw proclaims, "I am Heathcliff," Nora desires a similarity that transcends all external difference, sexual or otherwise—a likeness that implies her love includes a form of self-love that excludes difference and otherness.

Through these dreams Nora glimpses and thus gains access to herself in new ways. When she dreams of herself as asleep, she produces a figure of herself that is much like Robin. Robin is "la somnambule," the sleepwalker who is aware that she "belongs" to Nora, but it is also true that "if Nora did not make it permanent by her own strength, she would forget" (55). But whereas Robin half sleepwalks in order to half suffer, Nora struggles to be more awake regardless of the pain in the perhaps misguided belief that the history of her relationship to Robin can be changed, that a new story can be told. She both succeeds and fails, for part of what she must learn is that no matter how wide awake one becomes, there are limits to what one can know and what language can express—what one knows is always askew because of the imperfect correspondence between word and thing. What seems like truth to one is but a strange perspective to another, and the imposition of one's truths on others is a dangerous, violent, and ultimately unsuccessful enterprise. We cannot—and should not attempt to—control others' desires and behavior. Still, there are things Nora can and does learn: not everything is unknowable. For her to gain knowledge necessitates giving up the fantasy of herself as innocent. As Matthew says, "To be utterly innocent . . . would be to be utterly unknown, particularly to oneself" (138).

The power of the unknown is alluring. But to pursue it exclusively is to pursue perpetual innocence: it is to choose, by rejecting knowledge itself, to remain unknown to oneself in important ways. Perhaps the central contradiction in *Nightwood* rests here, in the power of the unknown to overturn virtually every form of knowledge—even epistemology as a human activity. This is ultimately a dangerous and repressive move. Matthew's discourse, because an infinite eking out of language, leads to confusion, to the compelling attraction of language as an embodiment of desire, to just this kind of embracing of the unknown. But Nora's goals are more pragmatic.

There is no end to the confusion in *Nightwood*, no final solution to the difficult questions the text asks about the possibilities available for subjects who resist oppressive and repressive cultural configurations with tremendous ambivalence and pain. It is as if the representations of differences in sexuality are constructed around a vortex which constantly threatens to suck all forms of human significance into its own emptiness. Nora resists its pressure, and in order to do so she must paradoxically rely on certain cultural forms that the text deconstructs, including psychoanalysis. Nora seeks to understand Robin's night world and to learn to speak her own story. "I'm so miserable," she tells Matthew. "I don't know how to talk, and I've got to. I've got to talk to somebody. I can't live this way"

(129). Matthew does not, however, play the classical analyst to
Nora's patient or priest to her confessor. Unlike the analyst who
listens but rarely speaks, becoming essentially a blank screen upon
which the patient projects fantasies, or the priest who listens in
silence, Matthew fills up the text with his own monologues, believing that Nora and others will find comfort, if nothing else, in the
distraction his speech offers. But even if his intentions are good, it
is Matthew who is thus comforted, though it may be more accurate
to say that like the others he is merely momentarily diverted. That
his speech relieves his own suffering is especially apparent when
his pain intensifies as Nora begins to discover her voice and insist
·upon more space for herself in their exchanges. Clearly this is the
scene of neither analysis nor confession. Rather, these exchanges
parody both psychoanalysis and confession. As Marcus points out,
in *Nightwood* the doctor's womb envy is so strong that it parodies
Freudian penis envy:

> The psychoanalyst's office is a filthy bedroom with a reeking
> chamber pot. Freud's famous totems, the sacred objects from
> ancient cultures that people his shelves and tables in H. D.'s
> famous tribute, are mocked by O'Connor's rusty forceps, broken
> scalpel, perfume bottles, ladies' underclothing and abdominal
> brace. The psychoanalytic structure is ruptured as the patient
> asks the question and the doctor answers. The doctor is in bed
> in a granny nightgown and wig, powdered and rouged, and the
> patient stands by his bed; it is three in the morning, not three in
> the afternoon. The patient is rational, Puritanical and analytical
> and the doctor is mad. ("Laughing" 233)

But madness is a concept to use with care here, and in some ways
the result of their exchanges mirrors the desired result of analysis.
Nora does learn how to speak and begins to give shape to what she
has hitherto been unable to put into words. If she is not "cured"—
for perhaps no cure is possible—she takes the authority of her own
experience more seriously.

Early portraits of Nora describe her as one whose need to control
her environment keeps her aloof. She is entirely nonjudgmental of
others; she neither reproaches nor accuses. But this is because she
keeps herself distant and different. While these qualities draw others to her, they also frighten them, for she merely reflects their own
images back to themselves. Unable to insult her or hold anything

against her, they are embittered at having to "take back injustice that in her found no foothold" (53). Her eyes are unseeing in that they impose a predetermined design on the chaos of experience: to others they are like "that mirrorless look of polished metals which report not so much the object as the movement of the object" (52). The world is as inaccessible to her as she is to it, for like the plays she attends it is "contracted and fortified . . . in her own unconscious terms" (52). As Nora herself is unconscious of the design she imposes on the world, she is unaware that it is a design at all. But in fact the "world and its history [are] to Nora like a ship in a bottle; she herself [is] outside and unidentified, endlessly embroiled in a preoccupation without a problem" (53).

Like Robin, Nora's preoccupation is her predicament, a predicament that seems to get resolved—or more accurately, turn into a different kind of predicament—by their contact with one another. Because their love exists beyond the prescribed categories of heterosexual culture, beyond the known and opposed to cultural prescription, it provides an impetus for change. Still, Nora and Robin are different as women and as lovers. Unlike Robin, Nora wants power and control. As she asserts, "And I, who want power, chose a girl who resembles a boy" (136). They each play a part that for a time locks them together in a circular psychological drama. Robin's distance and self-sufficiency produce in Nora a desire for more closeness and make her neediness more intense, which makes Robin even more distant.

Yet Robin is not altogether distant from her surroundings. In marked contrast to Nora's aloof distance at the events of high culture—at plays and operas—is Robin's proximity to the circus, the opposite of high culture. Here, animals all but climb out of the ring at the spot where she sits. The caged lioness makes the connection between Robin and the animals even more pronounced: she bows down and regards Robin "as if a river were falling behind impassible heat; her eyes flowed in tears that never reached the surface" (54). Not only does the lioness acknowledge some painful bond between them, the image of Robin and the lioness is the inverse reflection of Nora at the theater. The former is incomprehensible but made powerfully alive and poignant in the language Barnes uses to describe it. The latter is understandable but dead.

Shari Benstock argues that in "mapping the inversions and subversions of sexual difference under the law that would enforce heterosexuality, Barnes's work anticipates (and simultaneously puts into question) the Lacanian notion that heterosexuality unwrites the very law of difference it would seem to put into place. That is, heterosexuality in Western culture is really a form of what has previously been defined as homosexuality: as a search for an image of the self, a search for the twin, a search for confirmation of one's identity through the double, a reinforcement of *sameness* under the guise of difference" (247). Nora is unable to distinguish Robin from herself. And yet, as Benstock notes, Barnes questions the way homosexuality is defined by traditional psychoanalytic theory. Nora's desire is to a great extent structured and influenced by patriarchal, heterosexual law—it is impossible for her to step outside culture to attain an ahistorical homosexual love. At the same time, her experience takes her outside the known, to what has not yet been written (though the text itself makes a contribution to getting it written). Unlike her grief, the forms for which she can borrow from theater, her sexual contact with Robin has no public form to appropriate, leaving her entirely on her own.

In psychoanalytic terms Nora's love—like all love—originates in narcissism but is transferred to an overvalued love object. This puts her in a "masculine" position, for women, Freud argues, generally love only themselves. It is roughly in these terms that Matthew reads Robin's narcissism. For Matthew, the narcissistic woman is characterized by the need to be loved rather than to love, by self-sufficiency, and by beauty. According to Matthew, "Every bed [Robin] leaves, without caring, fills her heart with peace and happiness. She has made her 'escape' again. That's why she can't 'put herself in another's place,' she herself is the only 'position'; so she resents it when you reproach her with what she has done. She knows she is innocent because she can't do anything in relation to anyone but herself. You almost caught hold of her, but she put you cleverly away by making you the Madonna" (146). Here Robin seems characteristic of Freud's narcissistic woman, who is frightening in her self-contentment and self-sufficiency. For Freud, such a woman does not need man's desire to please and desire herself. What is attractive about such women is their ability to maintain a primary narcissism that men give up but remain nostalgic for. However, Nora challenges the authority of Matthew's interpretation, as in the passage previously quoted when Nora realizes she was not for Robin the Madonna (as Matthew suggests she was) but rather a "fixed dismay . . . the 'indecent' eternal" (157).

Along similar lines, Sarah Kofman challenges Freud's interpretation of the narcissistic woman. Kofman points out that Freud does not pursue what his analysis in "On Narcissism" opens up: the possibility of conceptualizing women as criminal outsiders rather than as hysterics. As a criminal, "woman is the only one who knows her own secret, knows the solution to the riddle and is determined not to share it, since she is self-sufficient, or thinks she is, and has no need for complicity" (66). Instead he chooses a way of thinking that soothes male egos, that says that a woman is "completely ignorant of her own secret, [but is] disposed to help the investigator, to collaborate with him, persuaded that she is 'ill,' that she cannot get along without man if she is to be 'cured' (66). Kofman states that at some level Freud knew otherwise, that women were—or conceivably could be—great criminals, not hysterics, but strove to "pass them off as hysterics, for it is very much in men's interest that women should share their own convictions, should make themselves accomplices to men's crimes, in exchange for a pseudo-cure, a poison-remedy, a 'solution' that cannot help being pernicious since it restores speech to women only in order to model it on men's, only in order to condemn their 'demands' to silence" (66–67).

In her proximity to the beast, her flagrant disregard of patriarchal, heterosexual values, and her "narcissism," Robin is a criminal outsider. She does not fit into psychoanalytic or other cultural categories, which is her disruptive strength. If she at times seems in collusion with oppressive social structures, she manages to break away—yet what she breaks away to seems alternately alluring and horrifying. If, as Kofman suggests, in a heterosexual society the demands put on female subjects to transfer their erogenous impulses from the primary love object (the mother) to the father produce the conditions that predispose women to neuroses and hysteria, such qualities are most evident in Robin when she's married to Felix and in Nora before she meets Robin. For it is then that the greatest repression is required by each. All this supports the idea that heterosexuality is a social but not a psychic norm. Robin and Nora are dissatisfied with the restrictive feminine sexuality that society encourages and sanctions; neither is neurotic nor hysterical in her playing of both "masculine" and "feminine" roles. In order to

be neurotic or hysterical, one must operate within the social contract and according to the rules where such terms apply, and with
Nightwood Barnes produces a context that displaces that social
contract. To the extent that either Robin or Nora is neurotic or hysterical, it is owing to being trapped between the confines of culture
and the destruction of that culture—to being in collusion, whether
consciously or unconsciously, with it.

With *Nightwood*, Barnes works to find a language capable of
breaking through to the other side of culture, to its destruction. Despite the contradictions and collusions in the text, to a great extent
she succeeds. But what *Nightwood* simultaneously demonstrates is
that it is virtually impossible to use language to represent an alternative that is not utopian without partaking in existing, sometimes
oppressive cultural configurations.

4 Marguerite Duras and the Subversion of Power

Thus far I have argued that the fiction of Virginia Woolf and Djuna Barnes sustains contradictory impulses and records ambivalence, for these writers challenge existing cultural norms while showing how female subjectivity and experience are shaped by these norms. At the same time, as part of the cultural phenomenon we call modernism but distinguished from the general movement in their representations of gender, desire, and power, Woolf and Barnes initiate among women writers new representations of female subjectivity and experience.

For Woolf, this enterprise is risky and transgressive and therefore full of ambivalence: her writing becomes a way to articulate and approach boundaries separating what Mary Douglass has called purity and danger.[1] But owing to her perceptions of social restrictions particular to women, her ideas about art, and her internalization of the treaty of silence that ensures the survival of marginalized and oppressed peoples, Woolf felt it would be impossible for her to write beyond purified, culturally legitimate territories into areas dangerous and transgressive. She tended to experience such restrictions most forcefully and ambivalently as internalized boundaries to be crossed only at her own peril. Having recognized these restrictions, she developed a lyrical prose style that, among other things, allowed her to resist being entirely contained by cultural boundaries. In this way, and without abandoning her idea of art, Woolf, much in the way Lily Briscoe in *To the Lighthouse* employs nonsignifying, rhythmic properties of language to complete her painting, discovers a form with which she can be subversive without crossing over entirely into the forbidden.

In contrast to Woolf, but as a woman writer who like Woolf attempts to represent female subjectivities in new ways, Barnes
stretches the lyrical aesthetic to include what lies beyond some of
the most firmly entrenched cultural restrictions and values. She
moves beyond purity to danger, to territories of subjectivity and experience excluded and repressed by culture. Such territories are
perceived by the dominant culture as dangerous and potentially
contaminating. Without Woolf's sometimes abstract and certainly
aestheticized form of resistance, Barnes writes explicitly and forcefully of taboos and transgressions with respect to subjectivity, violence, sexuality, and desire. She explores the violence of female desire. Any internalized constraints seem minimal indeed, given the
comparatively unrestricted way she writes of transgressive subjects. In *Nightwood,* violence and obsession, in combination with
highly stylized and theatrical prose, shatter conventional narrative
structure and representational strategies.

This is not to suggest, however, that Barnes produced a more
liberated subject or literary territory: her representations of sexuality, obsession, and violence show how subjects marginal to or outside the dominant culture still internalize its forms in ways that lead
them to be painfully in collusion with what is, after all, in their best
interest to resist or undermine. In this way, *Nightwood* represents
subjects who are contradictory. Moreover, *Nightwood* is contradictory in other ways too. As a critique of the dominant culture, *Nightwood* grounds itself historically in order to strengthen its subversive
resistance to a dominant, violent, and normalizing culture. But
Barnes's theatrical, performative prose also embodies an ahistorical
impulse—a desire to be liberated from the confines of society and
community—contradictory to the text's own historical imperative,
which is apparent in its painful representations of marginalized
groups who in one way or another lack cultural authority, including
Jews, lesbians, transsexuals, blacks, and circus people. And finally,
by pursuing the unknown for its own sake, the text embraces perpetual innocence and political naïveté.

Like Woolf and Barnes, Marguerite Duras represents ambivalence and contradiction. Like them, she produces nonpolemical
forms with which to shape essentially polemical subjects, focusing
on complex relationships among gender, sexuality, desire, the body,
loss, power, vulnerability, and violence—and, especially, on the implications of such relationships for female subjects. As Carol Mur-

phy notes, in Duras's texts poetic language produces a music that is "the language of desire and madness" (19). Like Woolf, Duras's prose has a diffuse, rhythmic quality that highlights language's nonsignifying properties. And like Barnes, Duras explores the violence of desire and the power of obsession. But unlike Woolf and Barnes, Duras translates these strategies into a distinctly postmodern practice. While attempts to distinguish modernism and postmodernism can be problematic, I mean simply that Duras's writing is self-reflexive. Duras's work is about female subjectivity, but it is equally about language and writing. More precisely, her texts are about the simultaneous success and failure of language and writing to represent female subjectivity and experience as they exist in the world. Duras represents subjectivities and bodies in and out of relation to language: language both shapes and fails to shape subjectivity in material life as well as in representations of subjectivity and the body. Duras's violent desire is a desire produced not only in social frameworks but in linguistic structures. Unlike Woolf and Barnes, then, Duras, is postmodern because in her representations of subjects and bodies she implicates language and writing explicitly in desire and eroticism, domination and violence.

In *The Politics of Postmodernism*, Linda Hutcheon points out that postmodernism is

> a critique both of the view of representation as reflective (rather than as constitutive) of reality and of the accepted idea of 'man' as the centered subject of representation; but it is also an exploitation of those same challenged foundations of representation. Postmodern texts paradoxically point to the opaque nature of their representational strategies and at the same time to their complicity with the notion of the transparency of representation. (18)

In other words, postmodernism responds to a crisis in representation, a recognition of language's mimetic failure, while it acknowledges the necessity of using language to represent the world, subjectivity, and experience. Postmodernism is, therefore, essentially and admittedly contradictory. It recognizes its own complicity with what it critiques; it recognizes that in order to make a critique at all it must participate in the forms of representation it simultaneously dismantles.

Duras's texts show how writing is connected to cultural power, for as we see most emphatically in *The Ravishing of Lol Stein* and *The Vice-Consul*, to write is to shape and control experience in symbolic ways. Even if language fails to represent the world "as it really is," discursive powers are more than symbolic: they have material effects because subjects constitute themselves out of existing and available discourses. But Duras, by producing textual terrains that are unstructured and uncontained by her own lyrical, associative, fragmented discourse, also shows how subjects exceed the structuring powers of language and culture. That is, she demonstrates how writing challenges normative, complacent attitudes about identity and meaning.

In Duras's texts, subjectivities are unstructured and uncontained. As productions of unstructured textual and psychological regions, these texts, especially *L'Amour* and *India Song*, employ desire to threaten the stability of the symbolic structures in language and the psychic structures of subjectivity. (I distinguish between these two productions of desire with the expressions "destructured" and "desublimated" desire, respectively.)[2] Like Woolf and Barnes, Duras writes toward the repressed of collective culture and individual subjects, but unlike them she shows that any attempt to write is threatened by the force of what exceeds representation.

In this way, and paradoxically given her own medium, Duras refuses to grant writing itself an unambivalent, noncontradictory kind of authority. She deconstructs the authority of her own writing: she dismantles her own positions in discourse and those of the speakers in her texts. With this deconstructive tendency and at a more abstract level, Duras replicates the ambivalent, contradictory positions apparent in the fiction of Woolf and Barnes. While her fiction insists on the imperative for radical social change, it undermines—to some extent, anyway—its own authority to assume a position from which experience can be represented in a meaningful way and on which action might be based. If her work cannot assert a position, its ability to intervene in sociopolitical contexts is limited. And this is, perhaps, one of the most basic contradictions in Duras's work for feminists, the feature that makes her writing seem at once subversive of and complicit with an oppressive discursive and material status quo. Feminism concerns itself with providing cultural positions for women, whereas Duras's texts take away those positions and demonstrate women's marginality in society and in discourse.

And yet, as Jane Gallop has written, feminism tends "to accept a traditional, unified, rational, puritanical self—a self supposedly free from the violence of desire" (xii). If Duras produces a kind of female subject marginalized in society and a femininity that is marginalized in discourse, she also unsettles feminism's more traditional notions of subjectivity and desire. In so doing she does not produce representations of women as they feel they ought or would like to be. Her work is in this way disturbing and provocative, for at this particular historical moment women are hungry for new and positive representations of what it means to be female.

Another disturbing feature of Duras's writing occurs because, despite the subversion of oppressive social codes and structures, the politics of her oeuvre is often rather astonishingly contradictory, at once subversive and repressive. For example, without any sense of regret or nostalgia, *Destroy, She Said* insists on the necessity to abandon conventional social and symbolic forms. From the perspective of normative cultural assumptions, its figures are frightening and perverse, even mad. This madness is, for the Duras of the 1960s, a desirable response to existing social conditions. Duras explicitly connects the text with social changes demanded by the student-worker uprisings in France in May 1968. "Capital destruction" refers, she says, to the

> destruction of someone as a person. . . . The destruction of every power. . . . The destruction of all police. Intellectual police. Religious police. Communist police. . . . The destruction of memory. . . . The destruction of judgment. . . . I am in favor of . . . closing schools and universities, of ignorance. . . . Of falling in line with the humblest coolie and starting all over again. . . . Please understand: we are all German Jews, we are all strangers. This is a slogan from the May revolution. We are all strangers to your State, to your society, to your shady deals. ("An Interview with Marguerite Duras" 108–109)

But while she here ostensibly endorses a position that, in its commitment to sweeping away so radically all past social, intellectual, and economic privilege, recalls the philosophy behind Mao's cultural revolution, Duras's lyrical prose style in her fiction is extraordinarily nostalgic and sorrowful. While insisting on textual spaces and subjects that are not contained or structured, these texts can hardly be said to celebrate unambivalently such open forms or lack of definitive, stable positions in discourse: as Winifred Woodhull notes, Duras's texts "call for a critical evaluation of non-positionality as a privileged notion in modern theory. Far from idealizing its subversiveness, her writing explores the culturally determined association of non-positionality with femininity and the ways in which this association contributes to women's marginality" (4). As different as Woodhull's assessment is from Duras's own description of her intent, neither position is unfounded. Duras's work is profoundly contradictory and invites a wide range of interpretations, while it resists being entirely contained by any unified perspective or theory.

In the midst of these texts without definitive positions, without traditional character, plot, and narrative sequence or order, Duras interjects political commentary. In *The Lover*, for example, Duras shifts from a lyrical description of the speaker and her brother playing—"I forget everything, and I forgot to say this, that we were children who laughed, my younger brother and I, laughed to burst, fit to die" (62)—to a recollection of meeting Robert Brasillach and Drieu la Rochelle, French fascists who collaborated with the Gestapo, at dinner parties (where politics was *not* a subject of conversation). Moreover, she reflects that their collaboration with the Nazis is exactly the same as her own later involvement with the French Communist party: "The parallel is complete and absolute. The two things are the same, the same pity, the same call for help, the same lack of judgment, the same superstition if you like, that consists in believing in a political solution to the personal problem" (68). By equating all political involvements, collapsing differences not only among various positions but among the reasons one might choose to become politically active, Duras seems to say that any kind of political involvement is misguided, rooted in a mistaken belief in political solutions to what she calls "the personal problem."

Even as it makes explicit political commentary, Duras's work insists on a distance between discourse and an inexpressible, radical exteriority in ways that subvert both material and discursive forms of power and control. The word or words that would guarantee meaning and produce an undeniable, seamless link between the material and the discursive and thereby grant authority to writing are always absent. In *L'Amante Anglaise*, the head, which has been cut off and which would provide a solution to the mystery of Marie-Thérèse's murder, is missing. Lol V. Stein suffers from the word that can't be spoken because it doesn't exist: "By its absence, this word ruins all the others, it contaminates them, it is also the dead dog on the beach at high noon, this hole of flesh" (38). The Vice-Consul insists he can do no more than assert that he finds it "impossible to give an account, in terms that would be understood, of what took place in Lahore" (27) when he shot indiscriminately into a crowd of suffering Indian lepers. Similarly, he cannot adequately express his feelings for Anne-Marie Stretter: "For what I want to say . . . there are no words" (98). Certainly it would be false to call what he feels "love," though his words repeat the conventional language of romantic love as it takes shape within the cult of romance and passion in the West. The question that no one can formulate properly, the missing head, the absent word, the inability of language to explain or to explore what matters most precisely because of its absence—all these factors subvert fixity and normative assumptions about language and culture. They also produce nostalgia, loss, and pain.

If these words existed, the origins of actions and foundations of subjectivity might be understood. But because they do not, origins and foundations are simultaneously inaccessible and intensely powerful, haunting, and desired because eternally absent. It is what cannot be said, what cannot be articulated using intelligible structures of thought, that results in this special kind of intriguing force. It also produces subjects without definitive shape: recognizable figures circulate among discrete texts with just enough variation to deny the fixity of a coherent, intelligible identity. Boundaries are blurred or collapsed, calling into question conceptual categories and distinctions between fiction and autobiography, image and language, pleasure and pain, gender and sexuality, the body and discourse, desire and writing. Duras's texts fashion a unique form of contradiction by simultaneously insisting on the coincidence and noncoincidence of such categories and distinctions. These texts are riddled with contradictions that stem from such a system of shifting equivalences, nonequivalences, and substitutions: fiction is fiction but also autobiography; a discrete text is self-contained but also inseparable from other texts in the Durassian oeuvre that "rewrite" the same scene differently; images are portrayed in language but exceed it; pleasure is the absence of pain but also its presence; gender informs sexuality, but sexuality exceeds the cultural construction of gender; the body is represented in language but drastically out of relation to it; desire is produced in writing but exceeds it.

In *L'Amante Anglaise*, language only inadequately represents fe-

male subjectivity and desire while emphasizing the radical split between itself and experience. This text, which subverts the traditional detective plot's assumption that motives for crimes can be
inferred and discovered with the appropriate evidence, insists that
the mystery of Claire Lannes—and the murder of her cousin Marie-
Thérèse that Claire is presumed to have committed—remains a
mystery. In the process of attempting to write a definitive account
of what happened, the writer's interest shifts from the crime to
Claire, who remains equally inaccessible and unknowable. *L'A-
mante Anglaise* is structured around three interviews with a writer
whose book (the text itself) is about to come into being. The text
self-consciously represents its own production, calling attention to
itself as a discursive construct out of relation to material practices.
It ostensibly moves toward a resolution of the mystery of Marie-
Thérèse's death by making each section's interviewee possess more
knowledge about Claire and the crime and by moving closer to, until finally ending with, Claire herself. But because Claire cannot
provide an authoritative explanation of the incident in an "appropriate" discourse, the resolution never comes. Claire cannot account for her behavior, though she teases the writer by suggesting
that if he would just ask her the right question, she could provide
the information he seeks. Such a question is not forthcoming. And
Claire wants to defer the ending, for as long as it is postponed the
detective writer takes a more intense interest in her than anyone
has for years. She is seduced when his interest in the murder turns
to an interest in her and wants to maintain the connection he
provides.

Claire can neither experience nor symbolize her life. If she mur-
dered her deaf-mute cousin, her action is really a symbolic suicide:
her aggression is aimed inward at her own passivity and her terribly
isolated, middle-class life without passion in a small rural town. If
Claire did murder her cousin, we must acknowledge that she had
no motive for *that* crime. Claire's action does, however, reproduce
the symbolic mutilation to which she is subjected. She is, in an
important sense, "headless" herself. Thus, by murdering Marie-
Thérèse she expresses her own fragmented state of subjectivity. If
this is, as Woodhull has stated, an attempt to "create the direct
equivalence presumed to exist between representation and lived reality" (11), the attempt fails since Claire's action is murder, not suicide. It would obviously be impossible for her to both decapitate and
dismember herself, a fact that stresses, in Claire's case, the impos-

sibility of bringing language and lived experience into alignment. Similarly, the title "L'Amante Anglaise" suggests Claire's inability to use language to adequately symbolize her experience. It transposes Claire's transposition: in a letter Claire writes "l'amante en glaise" (the clay lover) when she means "la menthe anglaise" (English mint), which indicates her radical distance from symbolic forms of expression. Duras's title combines one term from each expression to produce yet another configuration with a new meaning, "l'amante anglaise" (the English lover), which has no referent in the text since there is no English lover.

Claire's mistake connects writing, desire, and the body while stressing the noncoincidence among them, which Duras underscores with the transposed title. Although each phrase sounds the same when spoken, when written they signify differently. Claire, when writing for advice on how to grow "la menthe anglaise," her favorite plant, which she also sees as a means to cut the grease Marie-Thérèse uses in cooking, mistakenly writes "l'amante en glaise." Claire intends to find a remedy for the fat which saturates her body and for the similar congealing of her mind (she spends her days watching television). Her desires are just as stifled as they would be if they were literally saturated with congealed grease. As a lover, she has atrophied in her marriage, turned to clay. Her transposition reveals the extent to which her desire, her body, and her ability to write are all similarly bottled up. She turns to fantasies of passion—personal "solutions" to a more widespread social condition. As Duras makes clear, Claire is a representative female member of the community.[3]

Like Claire Lannes, Lol V. Stein is unable to symbolize her illness, experience, or desire, suggesting again the gap between language and experience. But whereas *L'Amante Anglaise* insists on a radical split between language and experience, *The Ravishing of Lol Stein* demonstrates the extent to which, despite this split, language nevertheless contains and shapes subjectivity differently for men and women. In this text, since it is narrated by a male doctor, Jacques Hold, who is obsessed with Lol, language reflects a particular kind of masculine perspective. Yet Jacques's unreliability and projections produce a gap between language and experience, since we see Lol through his distorting lens, which is marred by his own desires. To some extent Lol escapes being completely contained by his discourse: the extent to which she is subject to it shows that subjectivities and bodies are never absolutely out of relation to discursive practices and theories; the extent to which she escapes is a measure of the radical gap between them.

The contradictory claim Duras makes in these texts, that subjects are at once effects of discourse and exceed it, is reflected in contemporary feminist theory. One branch of feminist theory, often called Anglo-American, insists on the importance of recognizing sexual difference and the ways in which biological women are subjected to oppressive social conditions. The other branch, characterized by French feminists, focuses on the idea of "femininity" as produced and repressed in discourse. In *Marguerite Duras: Writing on the Body*, Sharon Willis notes that Duras's texts "inscribe the form of this contradiction" (14), that is, the contradictory noncoincidence between an essential femininity grounded in the body and the idea of femininity that is produced in discourse as an effect of that discourse.[4] As Willis points out, Duras's comments about her work imply a belief in an essential femininity:

> Referring to her own literary production, [Duras] comments: "We don't write at all in the same place as men. And when women don't write in the place of their desire, they don't write, they are plagiarizing" [*Les Lieux de Marguerite Duras* 102]. Duras repeats this conception of feminine writing in an interview published in *Signs*, where she associates women's writing with translation: "I think 'feminine literature' is an organic, translated writing . . . translated from blackness, from darkness. . . . The writing of women is really translated from the unknown, like a new way of communicating rather than an already formed language. But to achieve that, we have to turn away from plagiarism." (15)

But Willis adds that Duras's writing suggests a very different impulse: "These texts figure the impossibility of a discursive access to the real, while simultaneously forcing, through the pattern of breaches, of empty figures, our recognition that discourse is never out-of-relation to that unrepresentable real" (24). If we have no discursive access to the "unrepresentable real," to what exceeds and threatens culture, we cannot know, in the sense of being able to accurately conceptualize, what essential femininity might be—or, for that matter, anything else either. Thus, any attempt to represent female subjectivities, bodies, and desires differently and more authentically—without plagiarizing or imitating male desire as it is produced and privileged in representation and without replicating existing productions of female desire—is not only fraught with difficulty, it is quite simply impossible. Moreover, gender is always already produced in both material and discursive practices. The body is always already written on, making it extremely difficult to conceptualize and represent it differently in hopes of effecting social change.

Along these lines, Lol's suffering is problematic, for if she lacks subjectivity, it isn't altogether clear what the basis for her suffering might be. And if she lacks subjectivity, might she not in fact represent femininity as a discursive effect rather than a female subject in culture? As Jacques Hold asks, in a curiously ambiguous passage, "Mais qu'est-ce à dire qu'une souffrance sans sujet?" (*Le Ravissment de Lol V. Stein* 23), which I translate as, "What is one to make of a suffering without a subject?" In the Grove Press edition, Richard Seaver translates this passage as, "What is one to make of a suffering which has no apparent cause?" (13). But this translation loses the essential ambiguity of Duras's use of "sujet." The French throws both the cause of suffering and Lol's subjectivity into question: the absence of a subject suggests at once the impossibility of locating causal origins and Lol's absence as a subject. Given this ambiguity, as Jacques remarks, "to know nothing about Lol Stein was already to know her. One could, it seemed to me, know even less about her, less and less about Lol Stein" (72).

Duras's language produces a radical instability and contradictory meanings. If the origin of Lol's suffering is deeply problematic, what precisely constitutes her "ravishment" is just as confusing. In French, as in English, the word has several meanings, all of which resonate with Lol's story. It can mean rape or kidnapping—each a violation of a person's subjectivity, a taking away of integrity. But it can also mean transporting joy or delight: rapture. Unbothered by the resulting contradiction, Duras uses the term in both senses:

> M.D.   Maybe that's what life is: to enter within, to let oneself be carried along by this story—this story, well, the story of others—in a constant movement of . . . how do you describe it, when you're carried off from a place?
>
> X.G.   . . . abduction, ravishing.
>
> M.D.   Yes, that's what it is.

X.G.   It's this word "ravishing" that you used; one is "rav-
       ished" from oneself; one is "ravished" from others.
M.D.   That's what's best. That's what's most desirable in the
       world. (*Woman to Woman* 42)

Jacques believes that Lol is ravished the night of the T. Beach ball,
that she subsequently seeks out her own ravishment in her compulsive wish to repeat the moment of trauma, the moment when
she, heretofore the object of Michael Richardson's love and affection, is completely forgotten. In his terms, "ravissement" is not desirable. But the word works in ways he does not intend, over which
he has no control or authority, for in another sense Jacques ravishes
Lol by appropriating her story to his own psychic needs. And perhaps it is also the reader who ravishes Lol—at least to the extent
that he or she imposes, as Jacques does, an external framework
upon the unknowable space at the center of Lol's story.

If Lol is ravished, she also ravishes: she is both the subject and
object of the title. She transports Jacques away from himself, for
she takes him away from the person he was and thought he knew.
Appropriated by him, distorted by his projections and fantasies, she
remains inaccessible, second to his own desires, verbal pleasures,
and textual erotics. While the effect Lol has on the reader is probably not so intense, the text provides an imaginary transport for the
reader as well. It takes us away, as all writing does, from ourselves
into an unfamiliar terrain, while at the same time our own conscious and unconscious desires shape and produce the text. Perhaps, too, Jacques Lacan is right to suggest that it is *Duras* who
ultimately ravishes *us* with such a text.[5] She ravishes us with writing that is as provocative and alluring as it is violent and disturbing.

Indeterminacy produces a seductive effect that is at once diffuse,
alluring, and strange. It not only isn't clear when the story begins
or ends, it isn't even clear what the story is. In one sense, Lol's story
begins when she is abandoned by Michael Richardson at the ball.
But others believe the story really starts long before that. Tatiana
always believed Lol was different, not quite there, for she didn't ever
seem to suffer like other people. For Tatiana, the original moment
or event, the one that structures all that follows, does not exist. And
in yet another sense, possibly the most persuasive, Lol's story begins
ten years later, when she meets Jacques Hold, since the story we
have doesn't exist apart from his production of it. Actually, it is his

story—that is, about him—quite as much as it is Lol's. If this is the story of the "eternity of the ball in the cinema of Lol Stein" it is just as much the story of the eternity of Lol V. Stein in the cinema of Jacques Hold.

Along these lines, the text suggests that psychoanalysis is a male story—about men and male desires—with questionable and harmful effects on biological women. But it also resonates with certain aspects of psychoanalytic theory. In particular, Duras's work tends to be read frequently in the context of Lacanian psychoanalytic theory. Lacan's remark in response to *The Ravishing of Lol Stein*, that "Marguerite Duras knows, without me, what I teach" ("Homage to Marguerite Duras" 124), implies that the text illustrates his own theory and principles. His comment appropriates her work. And, given Lol's inability to symbolize her subjectivity or experience, it perhaps isn't all that astonishing a claim. As Lacan asserts, "There is woman only as excluded by the nature of things which is the nature of words, and it has to be said that if there is one thing they themselves are complaining about enough at the moment, it is well and truly that—only they don't know what they are saying, which is all the difference between them and me" (*Feminine Sexuality* 144). Yet, as the passage illustrates, Lacan's own discourse is often masterful and privileges the phallus, professing to be convinced of its own authority and veracity—and this kind of mastery is very much at issue in, and very much at odds with, Duras's texts.[6]

However, to claim that Lacan's discourse is masterful, phallocratic, and offensive is not to tell the whole story about Lacan. Lacan also insists upon the failure of the phallic order, a failure related to its inability to account for the feminine, for what is "other" to it. As Jane Gallop so cleverly puts it:

Not simply a philosopher, but, artfully, a performer, [Lacan] is no mere father figure out to purvey the truth of his authority; he also comes out seeking his pleasure in a relation that the phallocentric universe does not circumscribe. To designate Lacan at his most stimulating and forceful is to call him something more than just phallocentric. He is also phallo-eccentric. Or, in more pointed language, he is a prick. . . . the prick is both resented by and attractive to women. . . . this epithet astoundingly often describes someone whom women . . . despite themselves, find irresistible. . . . The prick does not play by the rules;

he (she) is a narcissistic tease who persuades by means of attraction and resistance, not by orderly systematic discourse.
(36–37)

Lacan's discourse, by exposing its own position and desire, undermines its own assertions of mastery and authority in a tantalizing
double gesture. Because Lacan dismantles his own position in this
way, refusing to allow his difficult and elusive discourse to become
fixed and seeking a pleasure beyond the boundaries of the pater-
nal order, he is, as Gallop acknowledges, both disturbing and attractive to many women. His lectures were certainly well attended.
Still, however ironic Lacan's discourse or performance may be, the
double response women have to "the prick" is perhaps not all that
different from many women's ambivalent response to the more traditional father figure. This ambivalence is one of the ways that, having been born into a society in which male authority dominates,
women enact their internalization of oppression and participate in
the reproduction of patriarchal values and institutions.

Lacan rewrites Freud in the context of linguistic theory and
maintains that since it is within language that the "I" must be pos-
tulated, and since it is within language that women are inscribed as
other, as negative difference, women's relationship to language and
thus culture is problematic.[7] If for male children the entry into culture entails an acknowledgment of loss and deprivation, for female
children this entry involves lacking this experience of loss, since
feminine positions in discourse are not subject positions. Therefore,
if language displaces the male subject it doubly displaces the female
subject, and the essential experience of culture is different for male
and female children. Identity within culture is always alienating,
but Lacan's framework suggests it is even more alienating for female subjects. Language precedes the subject and determines differences, equivalences, and instabilities. It "speaks" the individual
subjects born into it, while these subjects must use language to
negotiate their relationship to society and culture. To rediscover the
laws that govern this "other scene" is to discover the unstable elements of language and thus of subjectivity. Lacan's subject is not
split in the sense that in a different society it could be made whole:
it is created in a split, which produces the conditions whereby it can
begin to conceptualize itself at all. Thus, as Lacan puts it in a discussion of the phallus as transcendental signifier, that is, as "the

signifier intended to designate as a whole the effects of the signified, in that the signifier [the phallus] conditions them by its presence as a signifier" (*Ecrits* 285), "man cannot aim at being whole (the 'total personality' is another of the deviant premises of modern psychotherapy), while ever the play of displacement and condensation to which he is doomed in the exercise of his functions marks his relation as a subject to the signifier" (*Ecrits* 287). The phallus does not guarantee power and privilege in any essential way: to identify with the phallus is to acknowledge the radical instability of the "authority" and position of mastery it offers.

Lacan's subject conceptualizes itself in a radical split, in what Lacan calls the mirror stage. This representation of the subject to itself is an identification, a "transformation that takes place in the subject when he assumes an image" (*Ecrits* 2). The image the subject assumes is a fiction: it is not the subject itself but an identification with what it perceives others perceive it to be. Thus, as Lacan says, "the important point is that this form situates the agency of the ego, before its social determination, in a fictional direction, which will always remain irreducible for the individual alone" (*Ecrits* 2). The unconscious is shaped by this early splitting.

If the notion of a whole self or identity is a fantasy or fiction, so too is the idea of a stable sexual identity. If the unconscious is structured like a language, as Lacan claims, it is subject to the same instabilities: signification is the result of negative difference, where meaning is constructed according to what something is *not* rather than to what it is in itself. The man can be—and is—privileged because he is not woman, but he is not privileged because the phallus has any intrinsic value. The slippage that results because meaning and value cannot be fixed with any certainty undermines sexual identity. Sexuality is ordered in the symbolic but unstable in the unconscious. As Jacqueline Rose points out in her introduction to *Feminine Sexuality*, for Lacan sexuality belongs to the realm of masquerade.

Although Lacan's radical undermining of identity and essential sexuality seems to have much in common with Duras's representations, for Alice Jardine it is "nothing less than astonishing as an event" that Lacan has written about Marguerite Duras (172). Jardine notes that Duras is the only contemporary writer about whom Lacan has written. In addition, her novels are "the only writings by a woman consistently invoked by Lacanian analysts" (172).[8] Critical of Jacques Lacan's identification with the Jacques of the text and his remark that Duras was able to understand his theory without him, Jardine states that "for the feminist reader, this book written by a feminist has only one subject: Lol V. Stein" (175). Jardine's suggestion that feminist readers identify not with Jacques Hold but with Lol is supported by Duras's comment (itself rather surprising, I think) that many women have written to her of their powerful identification with Lol (*Woman to Woman* 117). Still, because Jacques's perspective almost entirely governs our relationship to Lol, any identification with Lol on the part of female readers is mediated through his masculine biases and desires. Jardine, along with other critics, glosses the apparent contradiction (that women are identifying not with a feminine potential for a new kind of subjectivity but with a woman who, to the extent that she is *known* at all, is produced by and is a response to male desire) by insisting that women readers are interested most in Lol (as if she existed purely or apart from Jacques's use of her), a move that resists the recognition that the text is essentially contradictory. After criticizing Jacques Lacan for identifying exclusively with Jacques Hold, Jardine suggests uncritically that feminist readings replicate what she has just faulted Lacan for.[9] She notes, however, that disparate readings are not simply the result of strict sexual identification. In Jardine's analysis of the criticism, it is nonanalysts who see in Lol the potential for a new kind of subject in the world and analysts (Lacan and Montreley are representative here) who see Lol as a trope dissolved by the real. While the body of criticism on Duras does not bear out this distinction between analysts and nonanalysts, what finally interests Jardine is the disagreement she believes is produced by two "machines of interpretation (feminist and psychoanalytic)" (176).

Because the text is Jacques Hold's unsuccessful attempt to control language and discourse—to produce a narrative that shapes Lol, tells her story, and provides an intelligible, truthful account of her madness—it is impossible to disentangle his projections from any "essential" Lol. The validity of Jacques's discourse is precisely what's at issue. Because he interprets Lol's madness as the result of her abandonment by Michael Richardson, her fiancé, Jacques glosses over clues Lol provides to the contrary that would necessitate a story different from the one he tells. For example, Lol insists that from the moment Anne-Marie Stretter walked into the room, she "ceased to love" Michael Richardson. Lol suggests that by the time of the supposed origin of her illness or madness, the early morning hours when the ball came to an end, she was no longer in a position to be abandoned—at least not by Michael Richardson. If Lol's desire shifts with the arrival of Anne-Marie Stretter, who in many of these texts evokes desire in all the figures who surround her, the implication is that Lol's desire has been redirected toward her. It is from a conventional perspective that Lol's desire seems directed exclusively heterosexually, toward Michael. But in the triangular configurations, which echo the original triangle among Lol, Jacques, and Anne-Marie Stretter, Tatiana Karl is as important to Lol as Jacques is: Lol's desire encompasses them both. It is not in this way directed or structured according to social codes, values, or conventions.

In one sense, Jacques's narrative strategy, as Martha Noel Evans argues in *Masks of Tradition*, evinces his reliability as a narrator. For Evans, Jacques's commentary on his own discourse produces credibility. But whether he professes to lie, invent, imagine, or report what he knows, his authority is also undermined by his inability to master or structure the story. The text subverts any credibility with its convoluted, fractured syntax, repetitions of whole sections of text almost verbatim (as if Jacques forgets what he's already reported),[10] comments revealing Jacques's own obsessive interest in Lol as illustrated by such remarks as, "On three occasions, Lol and I were the only ones laughing" (81), and admissions that entire blocks of text have been lies. This is the case in the following passage, when, from the window of the hotel room where he waits for Tatiana, Jacques spots a woman "about whose grayish blondness there could be no doubt whatsoever":

I had a violent reaction, although I had been prepared for any eventuality, a very violent reaction I could not immediately define, something between terror and disbelief, horror and pleasure, and I was tempted by turn to cry out some warning, offer help, thrust her away forever, or involve myself forever with Lol Stein in all her complexities, fall in love with her. I stifled a cry, prayed to God for help, I ran out of the room, retraced my steps, paced the floor like a caged animal, too much alone to love or not to love, sick, sick of my frightful inability to admit what was happening. . . .

I'm lying. I did not move from the window, my worst fears
confirmed, fighting back the tears. (109–110)

The rhythmic intensity in the passage steadily increases, approach-
ing melodrama, equating writing with desire, but loses its momen-
tum when Jacques admits that he lies. It is as if the possibilities
inherent in language to construct meaning, rather than the truthful
representation of events, govern his discourse. These "facts" put a
blunt end to his verbal erotics.

If Jacques Hold takes a more active position in culture and the
production of meaning than Lol does, a more active involvement in
what Lacan calls the symbolic as part of his function as narrator
and shaper, it must still be said that his own subjectivity is none too
stable. As Jacques wonders when he meets Lol, "What is there
about me I am so completely unaware of and which she summons
me to know? Who will be there, at that moment, beside her?" (96).
Lol is to Jacques what Anne-Marie Stretter is to Michael Richardson: a figure to whom he is drawn for no reason he can account for
rationally. After seeing Anne-Marie Stretter, Michael Richardson
simply changes: "It was obvious to everyone. Obvious that he was
no longer the same person they had thought he was" (7). Similarly,
when Jacques becomes aware of his attraction to Lol, he becomes
unknown to himself and others.

It isn't as if Lol recognizes something about Jacques that is nascent or hidden. When she picks Jacques from all the other men she
could have chosen, her choice "implies no preference"; he is merely
the "man from [S.] Tahla she has decided to follow" (103). The attraction is completely impersonal, having nothing to do with personality. It does not originate in a self capable of meaningful choice
and action. But it triggers something important in Jacques and
changes his relationship to the world by putting into play repressed
structures in his own psychic life:

Just as my hands touch Lol, the memory of an unknown man,
now dead, comes back to me: he will serve as the eternal Richardson, the man from [T.] Beach, we will be mingled with him,
willy-nilly, all together, we shall no longer be able to recognize
one from the other, neither before, nor after, nor during, we
shall lose sight of one another, forget our names, in this way we
shall die for having forgotten—piece by piece, moment by moment, name by name—death. (103)

This unknown man who will function as the eternal Richardson isn't Michael Richardson. Instead, he serves as the "eternal Richardson," that third figure in the triangle that is an essential to Jacques's desire. It isn't the memory of Tatiana, who from Lol's perspective is the most apparent third party in this triangle, that comes to Jacques at this moment. It is instead the memory of another man, a man desired by the woman Jacques desires. The Jacques who narrates this story does not represent the Jacques in the story as being significantly involved with Lol because her relationship with Michael Richard reminds him of an unknown man who is now dead. Yet this unknown man is here remembered or produced by the resemblance. It isn't clear that he has a basis in Jacques's material past; it isn't clear whether he ever existed. He becomes a linguistic possibility, however, who can be brought into existence given Jacques's new involvement with Lol, an involvement that produces change and thus leads to death.

Duras's writing explodes signification by showing how language both represents and is exceeded by its own representations of subjectivity. Such explosions interrupt narrative and threaten to overwhelm the subject, as in the following passage where Jacques first learns that Lol has watched the window of the hotel room where he and Tatiana meet. Her words destroy his ordinary ability to make the world seem somewhat coherent. What happens in language separates language from experience:

> She has just said that Tatiana is naked beneath her dark hair. That sentence is the last to have been uttered. I hear: "naked beneath her dark hair, naked, naked, dark hair." The last two words especially strike with a strange and equal intensity. It's true that Tatiana was as Lol has just described her, naked beneath her dark hair. She was that way in the locked room, for her lover. The intensity of the sentence suddenly increases, the air around it has been rent, the sentence explodes, it blows the meaning apart. I hear it with a deafening roar, and I fail to understand it, I no longer even understand that it means nothing. . . .
>
> The nudity of Tatiana, already naked, intensifies into an overexposed image which makes it increasingly impossible to make any sense whatsoever out of it.
>
> The void is statue. The pedestal is there: the sentence. The

void is Tatiana naked beneath her dark hair, the fact. It is trans-
formed, poured out lavishly, the fact no longer contains the fact,
Tatiana emerges from herself, spills through the open windows
out over the town, the roads, mire, liquid, tide of nudity. Here
she is, Tatiana Karl, suddenly naked beneath her hair, between
Lol [V.] Stein and me. The sentence has just faded away, I can
no longer hear any sound, only silence, the sentence is dead at
Lol's feet, Tatiana is back in her place. I reach out and touch,
like a blind man I touch and fail to recognize anything I have
already touched. (105–106)

In this remarkable passage, Lol's words produce Tatiana as immediately present and effect a change in Jacques's relationship to the
world by propelling him into a space quite unknown to him. It is so
disorienting that he is temporarily unable to connect with the
world: his discourse disintegrates while suggesting a radical exteriority that language can merely begin to approach but never entirely contain. The sense of this radical exteriority is produced by
splitting language and experience. But at the same time the passage collapses language and experience. Tatiana, at once merely a
word, a collection of sounds, a void that means nothing, is also im-
bued with a material force. She spills out not only over and within
language but over the material objects that surround Jacques—the
town and the roads. Language acquires a material force comparable
to the body. In the same way, the absent word becomes for Lol a
"hole of flesh" as material as the dead dog on the beach. And when
Lol cannot stop talking Jacques produces an image of her literally
vomiting words, expelling them as if they were rejected food or
nourishment, which, of course, in a sense they are, since the
"right" word, the one that could make Lol well, does not exist.

   Although at such moments language produces and collapses into
material effects, the body nevertheless exceeds discourse and its
symbolic constructions. There is a radical distance between language and material exteriority. This is made especially apparent
during Lol and Jacques's trip to T. Beach, when, in several instances, Lol emphatically denies his version of things, suggesting
that she is not merely a discursive effect or idea of femininity. For
example, Jacques asks: "Why don't you kill yourself? Why haven't
you already killed yourself?" Lol responds, "No, you're wrong, that's
not it at all" (159). Her refusals mark the extent to which she is not

equivalent to his production of her. It is perhaps here, in Lol's refusal to conform to Jacques's construction of her, that Duras holds out some hope for a female subjectivity that could be represented as being beyond the confines of male imaginings and desires—and perhaps even beyond the laws governing the linguistic scene.

In the final pages of the text, Lol seems increasingly distant from and indifferent to Jacques, more and more beyond the containing powers of his discourse. This distance is enhanced by her apparent ability to insert herself into the symbolic, to symbolize for the first time her own split subjectivity. She isn't a unified subject but one who is radically split, as she emphasizes when she gives herself two names: Tatiana Karl and Lol V. Stein. That Lol names herself, however, is significant and introduces a shift. No longer entirely excluded from representational practices and the production of meaning, Lol inserts herself into two positions: she becomes the woman who is desired and the woman who is excluded. By occupying two positions in the triangle herself, Lol finds a way to repeat the drama of the night of the T. Beach ball without having to be abandoned. Whereas Tatiana was the desired other in a couple, she is now, because of Lol, the third term in the triangle.

Lol's ability to represent herself in this divided way does not, however, solve the problem of the noncoincidence between language and experience. This gap still exists, even if she bridges it somewhat. To bring the two into alignment is, Duras insists, an impossible enterprise. And finally the text does not attempt to resolve the difficult questions it raises about whether an essential female difference exists or whether femininity is more appropriately understood as an effect of discourse. Asleep in the field of rye, Lol becomes an image of indifference. But given the unreliability of Jacques's discourse and his stake in containing Lol, one has to wonder whether she's really there at all.

In *L'Amour*, Duras "rewrites" *The Ravishing of Lol Stein* to insist even more emphatically on the noncoincidence between writing and experience. Abandoning a male narrator who is himself a figure in the text, Duras moves away from equating writing with culturally legitimate forms of power. Instead, she uses writing to subvert such power and in so doing approaches both a more radically destructured textual space and a more radically desublimated subject. Paradoxically, the effect is writing that seems contrary to its own representational status, for in a strange way it acquires a material force while it underscores its difference from materiality. This effect is produced because the writing so radically departs from conventional assumptions about fiction and representation.

L'Amour is so destructured it is virtually unrecognizable as part of the Lol V. Stein cycle. And yet the shifting triangular structures suggest the profusion of triangles in *The Ravishing of Lol Stein*; the wandering movements of the figures, motions without discernible directions or goals, recall Lol's wandering through S. Thala. Place, though barely distinguishable because so minimal in *L'Amour*, seems vaguely similar, and the images such as the dead dog on the beach even more so. Except for the return to the scene of the ball, the circulation of images and figures is implicit, minimal, and undeveloped. No one is named. The text promises to "name this man, the traveller—if by chance the thing is necessary—on account of the slowness of his steps, the straying of his look" (13–14).[11] It never does become necessary, though what might constitute necessity and why it would involve the way he walks or the way his look strays also isn't clear. But because the man's look strays, he recalls Jacques Hold and Michael Richardson, both of whom are described in such terms in other contexts.[12] The three central figures, though unnamed, are sexed bodies—two male, one female—in a textual terrain bordered by the sea, the sky, the sea wall, the river, and the town. The terrain lacks as much definition as the bodies lack identity or character. Within the textual space and in no particular order, the quality of light shifts, the sea rises and roars, a child cries, alarms sound, and the bodies move about, sleep, and occasionally make contact with one another. And what the figures say to one another seems simultaneously void of meaning and highly charged with a significance the reader can't begin to understand.

There is little sense to be made, and this is the point. To enter this space one must leave behind conventional habits of reading and ways of constructing meaning. Here there are no plot, characters, and narrative. Even if we're encouraged to see the parallels with Lol's story, these substitutions never quite work. When the traveler mentions the ball to the woman in connection with her first illness, she knows exactly what he's talking about. She remembers having married a musician after her illness (Lol too marries a musician) and having two children (Lol has three, all daughters). She tells the traveler that she fell ill a second time and that a man (her husband?

another lover? Jacques Hold? Michael Richardson?) has died. She sleeps on the beach while he revisits the scene of the ball alone (in *The Ravishing of Lol Stein* both Lol and Jacques return to the casino). Like Lol and Jacques, the traveler encounters an attendant who shows him the room where the ball was held. From within, the two men can see the beach and the woman sleeping. In the exchange that follows, the traveler, who admits that he doesn't know the woman's name, asks the attendant if he recognizes the woman sleeping on the beach. The attendant "dit un nom" (131), but we don't know what name he says. In any case, it is a name he invents.

L'Amour isn't a text that invites what film theorists call suture. That is, it provides little if any means by which the reader might momentarily forget that the text is a fictional construct. This text never seems like life; it offers no construction of how one might actually live; with no characters and no plot, it represents nothing. Because it is so radically other to cultural conventions and stories, it is able to produce figures who are not so much individuals as markers in an ever-changing textual terrain. With the individual subject shattered, the emerging figures are not human beings but geometric shapes resulting from connections among and between bodies that cannot be understood in conventional ways, much less articulated. These forms are perhaps more accurately understood as traces of shapes, for they lack the definition and fixity necessary to produce anything solid.

In this strange and minimal space, traversed primarily by the three figures, desire circulates somewhat randomly—that is, through the figures but without any identifiable source or destination. Yet in some ways desire is less than random, for it moves along heterosexual lines. This seems equally true in *Lol V. Stein* and *L'Amour*, despite the differences in the extent to which structure and control are produced in each.[13] While the three figures of *L'Amour* do not desire in the way Jacques Hold does, the existence of a third party, the surplus of the extra male figure, triggers desire. But desire is not steady or consistent: the triangle first consolidates among the three figures on the beach, but it "warps and reshapes itself, never breaking apart" (8). This slippage within the triangle causes the man who just stands and looks to begin to walk, like the other man who walks up and down the beach, which sometimes produces confusion as to who is who. The movements of these figures apparently result from the force produced by the relations among their bodies—whether they move or remain where they are is determined by these relations, not by conscious control or volition. Their actions and desires originate in some unknowable place.

By taking bodies and desires out of the realm of discursive control, *L'Amour* takes the Lol V. Stein story almost completely out of the realm of individuality and identity. *L'Amour* is, as a result, also out of the realm of psychoanalytic theory as a discourse that attempts to explain how subjectivity comes into being. In fact, it resists assimilation to any such cultural theory or discourse, for, unlike *The Ravishing of Lol Stein*, it does not provide enough structure or control to allow for collusion with oppressive structures. Therefore, of the texts discussed here, *L'Amour* most completely destructures and desublimates desire in order to produce radical exteriority. What it sacrifices in order to do so is not only relevant social or political commentary but a discernible relevance to the world. If the space it produces is outside traditional configurations of power, because it dismantles structures of human significance and meaning in order to suggest a desire existing apart from cultural trappings, its ability to subvert such configurations is quite limited.

In contrast, *The Vice-Consul* puts the representation of desire and the noncoincidence between the body and language into a broader political and historical context: it dramatizes white European oppression of India, a particular historical situation, as a horror that cannot be articulated because it is simply unthinkable. This is not, or not entirely, because of an unbridgeable gap between language and experience but because extreme pain resists verbal articulation in special ways. If *The Ravishing of Lol Stein* dramatizes the effects of Lol's inability to symbolize her suffering and Jacques Hold's unsuccessful attempt to translate the story of her suffering into an authoritative discourse and *L'Amour* asks what a text without traces of social or cultural power might look like, *The Vice-Consul* underscores how the ideology of colonialism is deployed in ways that produce terrible forms of pain and oppression. It returns to the scene of Duras's experience in French Indochina. And *The Vice-Consul* precedes *L'Amour*: the emphasis on the social and political is not, as was the case with Woolf's response to *The Waves* in *Between the Acts*, a move from the abstract to the particular. Because *The Vice-Consul* insists on the reality of pain and oppression beyond its own boundaries, its position on the relationship between language and experience is necessarily different from the extremes of *L'Amour*. In order to insist on the existence of widespread pain, Duras must return to concrete particulars. At the same time the text foregrounds its fictional status, insisting at once on its separation from and relation to lived experience. It begins with Peter Morgan's story of the beggar woman's journey from Cambodia to Calcutta: the first line reads, "She walks on, writes Peter Morgan" (1). The text represents the miseries of imperialism while averring that representation itself is a form of imperialism.

The Vice-Consul takes place in Calcutta, where the white European colonials are surrounded by the unspeakable misery of hunger, leprosy, and madness, and on an island retreat in the Delta, where there are a luxurious European hotel and the French ambassador's villa. Anne-Marie Stretter, for whom Michael Richardson abandoned Lol V. Stein the night of the T. Beach ball, now married for seventeen years to the French ambassador, reappears and in this new context is connected to the "symbol of emaciated Calcutta" (118), the mad beggar woman of whom Peter Morgan writes. Michael Richardson "reappears" as Michael Richard. Anne-Marie is also strangely connected to the Vice-Consul of Lahore, who has committed atrocious murders and is now ostracized from the rest of white society. These three individuals form a textual center that alternately links writing with desire, domination, and death.

Anne-Marie Stretter is unable to give symbolic expression to her pain. In this respect she is much like other Durassian women, including Claire Lannes and Lol V. Stein, but also like the beggar woman who cannot, owing to her madness, even experience let alone represent her pain. Anne-Marie Stretter, like the beggar woman and the Vice-Consul, is mad. Suffering leads to the breakdown of psychic structure and intelligibility: Anne-Marie Stretter absorbs the pain of India in ways that cannot be verbalized. She embodies pain: "I cry for no reason that I can explain. It's as though I were shot through with grief. Someone has to weep, and I seem to be the one" (158). As a result, she seems "at home in this nightmare town" in ways others do not (85). Her pain and madness are the most appropriate responses to such a nightmare. For her, "contrary to popular belief, life [in Calcutta] isn't easy, it isn't hard, it's nothing" (85). Or, as she tells the Vice-Consul: "If one stays, since one can never see things as they really are, one has to . . . contrive, yes, contrive a way of looking at them" (92). All the whites feel oppressed by the suffering that surrounds them, and yet, with few exceptions, they seem to think along the same lines as the ambassador, that the situation can be made tolerable, that their "nervous tension" can be cured.

Elaine Scarry argues in *The Body in Pain* that, in contrast to mental pain which can be verbalized in psychoanalysis and in some ways eased, physical pain cannot be put into language; it actually resists articulation or translation. She notes that torture, for instance, is used at particular historical moments by unstable governments or powers in order to break down the experiences and narratives of those who oppose them. This happens when the stories of the opposition are too threatening to their tenuous hold on power. They destroy, therefore, the victims' ability to use language. The white Europeans of *The Vice-Consul* are certainly not torturers of the sort Scarry describes, but they are surrounded by human misery of such unspeakable proportions that it does indeed break down language. In such misery, one, like the beggar woman, has no story to tell: the structures that constitute one's world have collapsed. We cannot know if she even experiences pain, for she lacks the ability to represent it.

In order to maintain their own sanity, power, and privilege, all of which are virtually inseparable in this context, the white Europeans must learn to ignore what is beyond reason, beyond endurance. In this, their culture offers protection and guidance. Unlike the marginalized figures Barnes represents in *Nightwood* who are disenfranchised, the Europeans at the core of Duras's story enjoy almost unlimited power. Walls and fences separate India and the Indians from the luxurious European hotels and embassies. The Indian servant who wakes the "master" (in this case Charles Rossett) from his dream of a woman reading Proust is perceived as a "face with a sly expression [peering] cautiously through the open door" (33). Neither can see the other as entirely human. The one is "master," the other a face—a part not a whole. With the image of a woman reading Proust, and in conjunction with representing Peter Morgan as a writer, Duras suggests that only the privileged few have the leisure requisite to enjoy "the pleasures of the text." In light of the misery which surrounds them, such cultural pursuits on the part of the Europeans seem almost profane. For Charles Rossett, the dream provides a temporary escape from an unbearable reality.

By firing into a crowd of sleeping lepers, the Vice-Consul makes clear just what the European position in India entails. The act is beyond redemption, a refusal of what his culture professes to value above all else—human life. It is madness, but in a way, the Vice-Consul merely does what at some level they all want to do: eliminate the misery, perhaps for their own sake as well as for those who suffer. The Vice-Consul's action, however, is contradictory. It makes clear that the situation, the reality of his privilege and power and of others' pain, is beyond redemption: it cannot be changed by any one person for it is too overwhelming. But his actions also reek of supreme arrogance and power. He makes abundantly clear that all the whites have the power to end human life should they choose. As the ambassador asks, Who is there to care about Lahore? No one. So the colonizers have an unlimited, terrible power.

The figures of Anne-Marie Stretter and the Vice-Consul become equivalent because they both refuse to be blind to or repress the monstrosity of their positions as white colonizers.[14] And yet, within the white colonial culture, their positions could hardly be more dissimilar: she forms the center of desire, he its antithesis. As the wife of the ambassador, she enjoys power and status. The Vice-Consul, removed from his post, his future uncertain, has no status and no social position. Any connection between them is unthinkable from the perspective of white European colonial society. Ostracized by the whites, the Vice-Consul is cast out, forgotten, and ignored in the same way they try to ignore or repress the violence of India. In the fragile oasis of opulence amid extreme poverty, everything that enters the carefully planned world they've created for themselves must be made safe and acceptable, like cocktail party conversation. Surfaces must be maintained, and so the others resent the Vice-Consul because he forces them to notice him—just as they resent being forced to see the incredible pain that surrounds them.

Peter Morgan, the young male who writes the story of the beggar woman, represents public opinion and conventional morality. It is Morgan who steps in gallantly to remove the Vice-Consul from the embassy after his embarrassing outbreak of emotion for Anne-Marie. As he does so, he remarks callously that "a man of your sort is only interesting in his absence" (116). He denies all human connection with or compassion for the Vice-Consul; he denies this other's subjectivity and independence by controlling him. Signifi-

cantly, this is precisely what Morgan does in writing the story of
the beggar woman of Calcutta. On the way out to the island, Morgan describes his project to the others who, except for Anne-Marie
Stretter, are willing to contribute their opinions about how her story
should be written. Morgan wants to dwell on her filth: "She is
as dirty as nature itself, it's incredible. . . . Oh! I want to dwell on
that, her filth compounded of everything, and for a long time now
ingrained in her skin, a compound of the skin itself. I want to analyze her filth, describe what is in it: sweat, river-mud, scraps of
stale foie-gras sandwiches from your Embassy receptions, dust, tar,
mangos, fish-scales, blood, everything. I want to disgust you" (145–
146). As Michael Richard points out, what Morgan means "is something even more extreme. He wants to deprive her of any existence
other than her existence in his mind when he is watching her. She
herself is not to feel anything" (146). In short, writing her story
becomes a way of controlling her for his own purposes and desires.
Because like the Vice-Consul the beggar woman is interesting to
Peter Morgan only in her absence, not only is the Vice-Consul
linked with Anne-Marie Stretter, he is linked also with the mad beggar woman. They are all three interesting to write about—but terrifying to get close to.

On the trip to the island in the Delta, Charles Rossett, who was
selected the night of the party to be Anne-Marie Stretter's next
lover, discovers just how terrifying she is, at least from his conventional point of view. He tries to apply his own normative, romantic
ideas about how things should work between them and finds she
resists them. When he kisses her, he is shocked by a jolt of pain, for
she, like the Vice-Consul and the beggar woman, is like death. The
island, supposedly a much-needed retreat for white Europeans from
the misery of Calcutta, becomes a place of almost surreal horror for
Rossett. He realizes just how little he can control Anne-Marie Stretter, and, despite her choosing him as a lover, how little she desires
him. Moreover, he begins to realize that, regardless of appearances,
she really does desire the Vice-Consul. That this other man could
be the object of anyone's desire, given who and what he is, is simply
beyond his ability to imagine: "Oh! it's true," he says, "it's impossible, it's absolutely impossible to dwell on . . . the fact of his existence. . . . How can one possibly feel human affection of any kind
for the Vice-Consul of Lahore?" (155). When he realizes that Anne-
Marie's husband will have the Vice-Consul transferred out of Cal-

cutta because of the force of her desire, he is stunned: "You see," she says, "if I were to force myself to see him, Michael Richard would never forgive me. Nor, for that matter, would anyone else. I can only be the person I am here with you by . . . frittering away my time like this . . . don't you see?" (155). Anne-Marie Stretter's choice of Charles Rossett as her lover is utterly incidental. She has no real desire for him: he is a means for her to fritter away her time, a distraction that enables her to continue an impossible life. When he realizes this, his own desire is thwarted. It is not impersonal choice that he wants; in fact it challenges his way of life and what he values. He wants to be chosen for who he is, but Duras refuses this notion of personal choice.

Although Rossett attributes his loss of desire to her tears, the reasons are much more complex and are related to his unarticulated desire to possess and control—and to his immense frustration when he realizes she cannot be possessed. After she weeps, she goes not to him, whom she has just kissed, for comfort but instead to Michael Richard. At that moment Rossett realizes the truth of the Vice-Consul's words: "She's a woman without . . . preferences. That's what counts. You or me" (136). Like Lol V. Stein, then, Anne-Marie Stretter's choice is impersonal. And unlike Jacques Hold, Charles Rossett cannot accept this refusal to acknowledge his own individuality.

The complexity of Rossett's response to Anne-Marie Stretter, the extent to which he cannot articulate either what happens or his own response, is suggested in the following passage:

> He stops in his tracks, arrested by the memory of Anne-Marie Stretter's tears.
>
> He sees again Anne-Marie Stretter, rigid under the electric fan—in the heavenly rain of her tears, as the Vice-Consul might say—then suddenly the picture changes. There is something he wishes he had done. What? Oh! how he wishes he had raised his hand. . . . His hand is raised, it is lowered, it begins to stroke her face, her lips, gently at first, then more and more roughly. She bares her teeth in a painful contortion of a smile. More and more she surrenders her face to the impact of his hand, until it is wholly in his power. She is his willing victim. Slapping her face, he cries out that she must never weep again, never, never. She seems at this point to be losing her memory. No one is cry-

ing now, she says, there is nothing left that needs understanding. The slapping continues, more and more regularly. It is close to attaining rhythmic perfection. Anne-Marie Stretter, all of a sudden, is endowed with sombre beauty. Her heaven is being torn down, but she is resigned to it. Smoothly, with marvellous grace, her head moves. It is an effortless movement, as though her head were attached to her neck by a system of carefully oiled and incomparably intricate wheels. It has become, under Charles Rossett's hand, a living instrument.

Michael Richard was watching them. (161–62)[15]

By imagining her as a "willing victim," with Michael Richard standing by as witness and voyeur, watching him take control, Rossett fantasizes he is able, using violence, to make Anne-Marie Stretter into what he wants her to be, a "living instrument" to serve his own desires. As a representative of a certain kind of conventional male figure, Rossett is really more like the Vice-Consul than he might imagine, at least at the level of desires not articulated or known. In this passage his desire to dominate becomes clearer, his rage directed outward toward a weaker other. Like the Vice-Consul, he strikes out in order to assert some power over a misery which he cannot—outside of his own imagination—control. Having to some extent repressed his own pain, having refused to become like Anne-Marie Stretter a porous surface that absorbs the misery of the world, Rossett must forceably keep his protective psychic structures intact.

When Charles Rossett leaves Anne-Marie Stretter's island villa, that area of the island "fenced in for his greater protection" (161), he finds he must traverse a territory even more frightening than that he has just left, for this territory has not been fenced for white Europeans' protection. It is precisely what he thinks he cannot endure—madness, the breakdown of the symbolic order—that threatens him, both at Anne-Marie Stretter's villa and here. Because they are uncharted, the protected areas turn out to be almost as terrifying as the unprotected areas. It is outside in the truly uncharted, uncontrolled space that he encounters the mad beggar woman. Despite the disparity in their social status, the encounter terrifies him. The beggar woman bites off the head of a live fish and advances toward him. In this encounter his guarantees of power—his gender, race, language, and money—do him no good, for they will not serve here as currency. She refuses to acknowledge any of them. The beggar woman does not stoop to pick up the money he throws at her. Refusing his currency, which means nothing to her, she chases him to the hotel, then returns to the sea to pursue other prey.

Duras suggests with this encounter the elaborate cultural supports required to keep the institutionalization of white male power intact. One on one, Charles Rossett has no advantage. With the symbols of the power and privilege of Europe behind him, he does. In fact, it takes only reaching the Prince of Wales Hotel to bring him back to his senses—back to the realm where he can believe in his ability to understand what is happening to him. But with the madness that exists outside this at once fragile and powerful boundary, Duras points to the tenuousness of sanity. The borders between sanity and madness blur. There is much more that is not understood than is understood in the world; what is not understood is perceived as madness, as a threat by the figures who are most conventional.

If Anne-Marie does not allow herself to become Rossett's willing victim in quite the way he imagines, and if she seems in control when she instigates the Vice-Consul's removal from the embassy, it would not be fair to say that in other ways she escapes being precisely what these men want her to be—in Rossett's words, she is indeed a "living instrument." She embodies the pain of India while she serves as a conventional image of feminine grace and beauty in the midst of horror. She is a distraction from the horror as well as a reminder of it, for she is a figure who will take on everyone's pain. In the summary accompanying *India Song*, a text-script-film that repeats and reworks elements of *The Vice-Consul*, Duras describes Anne-Marie Stretter as born of the horror of "famine and leprosy mingled in the pestilential humidity of the monsoon": "She stands in the midst of it with a grace which engulfs everything, in unfailing silence—a grace which the voices try to see again, a grace which is porous and dangerous, dangerous also for some of them" (146). As much as anything, she is an image of Duras's writing, which could easily be described in precisely these terms. In the midst of horror, personified by the beggar woman who exists outside the boundaries of culture and sanity, Anne-Marie Stretter seems graceful, lyrical, and desirable. But Anne-Marie Stretter is not only linked with the beggar woman, she is in fact inseparable from her. Similarly, Duras's writing ravages: the combination of such intense beauty and

pain produces something like vertigo. Emotionally and intellectu-
ally, one reels from such prose, so "porous and dangerous." Like
Rossett, a reader enters a strange landscape where conventional
and rational structures no longer apply. It is a place alluring and
violent.

The Vice-Consul equates writing with violence and danger: it
refuses to purify writing, insisting instead on its terrible powers.
As Peter Morgan distances the beggar woman with prose by making her represent what he wants her to represent, so too does
Charles Rossett attempt to distance Anne-Marie Stretter by rewriting his involvement with her to enhance his own strength and
power, to assert his difference from her. Their actions mirror the
Vice-Consul's more outrageous act of violence against unknown
lepers. Given these rough equivalences, Duras suggests that the
impulses behind representation can be violent and brutal. Both
Morgan and Rossett want to distance themselves from others whom
they have a great psychic investment in seeing as radically different
from themselves. In *Powers of Horror*, Julia Kristeva explains the
desire to distance oneself in this way as a desperate attempt to avoid
weakness by connecting the frightening other with the concept of
abjection. To be abject is to be neither subject nor object: to refuse
this nonpositionality where boundaries blur is to assert one's own
position as subject, to reproduce boundaries and limits.

Because local passions get played out at a global level, *The Vice-
Consul* makes a more pointed political statement than many of Duras's other texts. Still, the force of its critique is tempered by the
allure of what always remains indeterminant. The magnitude of
this unknowable otherness continually threatens any position the
writing asserts, making the implicit political imperatives of the text
tempered by the power of fascination. Like Anne-Marie Stretter,
this writing is poised at the center of eroticism and death.

In *India Song*, Duras translates this powerful fascination into
film. *India Song* rewrites but does not cancel out *The Vice-Consul*,
much in the way *L'Amour* rewrites but does not cancel out *The
Ravishing of Lol Stein*. By rewriting in this way, Duras does not
correct the earlier texts, she extends them, producing intertextual
cycles that undermine the idea that a text is contained by its own
boundaries. *India Song*—at once a text, script, and film—is not,
however, as minimally structured as *L'Amour*. Still, like *L'Amour*, it
abandons figures of writers or narrators who attempt to control or

shape the material. Even Voice 4, who remembers the most about the texts which form the backdrop to *India Song*, does not deploy that knowledge in order to gain authority or mastery. By rewriting *The Vice-Consul* as *India Song*, Duras produces a sense of the impossibility of ever getting the story right. Instead, it is necessary to tell it again and again. In *The Vice-Consul*, Michael Richardson of *The Ravishing of Lol Stein* becomes Michael Richards. In *India Song*, he is Michael Richardson once again. It isn't clear at the end of *The Vice-Consul* that Anne-Marie Stretter intends to kill herself (or if she actually does), whereas in *India Song* this is established as fact right from the beginning in the plot summary Duras suggests should accompany all productions. In *Indiá Song* sirens are heard in the background, recalling *L'Amour*.

There is a radical separation between the voices, who speak of the story being enacted as well as of the incidents that precede that enactment, and the figures and images of which the voices speak. The voices are overwhelmed by their own fascination with what they observe and remember: they speak of their own responses to what they see and try to remember what has happened. They become another story apart from the action of the stage, screen, or text. It is, as Duras writes in her notes, Voice 1's fascination that frightens Voice 2, for the speakers of these voices are lovers and involved in their own passion.[16] The voices' responses reveal as much about them as about the story they remember. In this intertextual series of substitutions, each voice remembers the story in ways that fit his or her own psychic needs. The story they recall is not "a" story at all but fragments of the various texts. Superimposed on such images as Anne-Marie Stretter's breast that resist assimilation to the symbolic structures of their discourse, the voices seem closer to the reader or viewer and less fictional.[17] Because they treat the figures in the story as if they too were real, these fictional figures from the texts seem to cross the boundary separating writing and experience.

The interplay between the voices' rhythms, their silence, the other sounds, and the images produces a deep melancholy. Nothing connects perfectly or falls into place. What remains is longing and desire. No one voice or perspective has authority or attempts to impose its version of the story on the others, though Voice 4, spoken in the film by Duras, remembers the most and so helps Voice 3 to remember. All four voices are enchanted with what they have been unable to forget from the other texts in the Lol V. Stein cycle. What becomes important in *India Song*'s rewriting of *The Vice-Consul* is passion: the terrible desire between Anne-Marie Stretter and Michael Richardson overshadows the political commentary of *The Vice-Consul*. In this text, individual emotion is all. It distracts the voices from their own situations or makes those situations more intense. It threatens to absorb and dissolve all forms of rationality, coherence, and significance. Writing is, therefore, not exactly out of relation to subjectivities. It captivates and fascinates. Shot 22 shows "Anne-Marie Stretter's nude breast, surrounded by the black peignoir. Beads of sweat form on the skin as she breathes" (Lyon 23). Lyon states that the image of the breast is about a "fantasy of looking . . . [which] could be said to be the desire to see loss, to see what is by definition that to which the subject can have no access, but through which, at the same time, the subject is marked" (25). For Lyon, the image of the breast traces the middle ground between voyeurism and melancholia, a place where the subject is both excluded and included.

Just as they captivate the voices in *India Song*, Duras's texts captivate their readers. As Kristeva argues, Duras's texts seize us and draw us to "the dangerous brinks of our psychic life" ("Pain of Sorrow" 151). According to Kristeva, these texts "should not be given to fragile readers, male or female. . . . There is no purification at the end of these novels laden with disease, no heightened sense of well-being, no promise of a beyond, not even the enchanting beauty of style or irony that would provide a bonus of pleasure beyond the ill revealed" (140–141). She advises the frail to see Duras's films or plays instead, where the pain is diminished, concealed by a "dreamy charm" that makes them more conventional and artificial. For Kristeva, Duras's texts cultivate the mental and spiritual malaise of the postmodern world—the result of tremendous upheavals in the twentieth century in virtually every facet of cultural, social, spiritual, and political life. Duras's work does not attempt to console or cure—it writes toward a space in which cure is impossible and irrelevant. It does not provide a way to avoid, defer, or experience a cathartic release of psychic pain. As such, to some extent it is the opposite of clinical discourse that would attempt to provide some consolation, compensation, or cure.[18]

Because antithetical to clinical discourses that serve explicit, if sometimes oppressive, social functions, Duras's writing practice and her representations of herself as author contrast with the other writers she represents in her texts: the reporter in *L'Amante Anglaise*, who wants to find out what happened to the head so that the entire female body can be reassembled, the narrative constructed, and Claire Lannes understood and subsequently forgotten, and Peter Morgan, who attempts to control and distance the beggar woman. For Duras, an essential part of the resistance to oppressive forms of convention and tradition involves her refusal as a writer to overdetermine and control her texts, her refusal to participate in writing that dominates its subjects. In this sense, as Marcelle Marini has argued, Duras's work explores territories coded as feminine and excluded by a masculine symbolic. Lol V. Stein remains inaccessible to Jacques Hold, and Anne-Marie Stretter to Charles Rossett, whom she prefers only in the most impersonal way. The beggar woman of *The Vice-Consul* exists in a radical exteriority just as much as in Peter Morgan's narrative, for his narrative does not produce the entire text. And in *L'Amante Anglaise*, Marie-Thérèse's missing head, despite the writer's persistence, is never found. All these events suggest the impossibility of coherence or wholeness—not just of the body but of writing and of texts. What these figures attempt to control is often exactly what eludes them, for no matter what their intent, in Duras the "head" is never among the other pieces.

Duras refuses to "possess" her texts. When Xavière Gauthier asserts in *Woman to Woman* that anyone can "possess" these texts because they don't belong just to Duras, Duras agrees that they belong to the reader—there are as many Lol V. Steins as there are readers. According to Duras, the best thing a critic ever said about her work was when Kevork Kuttakdjian told her that *he* was the one who had written *The Ravishing of Lol Stein* (*Woman to Woman* 144). That Duras should love it when someone would say such a thing seems strange but is connected to a writing practice that attempts to map out terrains where individual mastery and control no longer have significance or value.

With *The Lover*, Duras represents herself explicitly as a writer unwilling to assert definitive control over the material. In some ways this gesture recalls Woolf's representations of Lily Briscoe and Miss La Trobe, female artists who challenge assumptions and attempt to find new forms. But if Woolf was trying to find forms that would make new representations of subjectivity and experience

possible, Duras questions the enterprise of representation altogether. While it is a work of fiction, not autobiography, *The Lover*
blurs such distinctions: the woman in the text seems much like
Duras. Duras claims it as her "true autobiography," and indeed
many of the woman's experiences in *The Lover* parallel events we
recognize from Duras's own life. Like Duras, the speaker grows up
in Indochina. Like Duras, the speaker is French; she is a writer;
she has a son; she has two brothers, the younger of whom dies
during the war from lack of medication; her mother is a teacher;
her father dies when she is quite young; she leaves Indochina to
attend school in Paris; she drinks "too much" in middle age; and
she is roughly the same age as Duras. Moreover, the front and back
jacket photos of Duras herself, which also appear in a text she published with Michelle Porte, *Les Lieux de Marguerite Duras*, seem to
be presented as photographs of the speaker in *The Lover* when she
was young. The speaker describes, for example, the fedora that
seems to contradict her small, puny body. Duras wears such a hat
in the back jacket photo, and Duras is physically a very small person. Since *The Lover* is at least in part inspired by autobiographical
material, one might reasonably expect it to bridge the gap between
writing and experience, for Duras is writing about experiences
in the world. But such is not the case. Instead of bringing writing
and experience into alignment, the text portrays the two as related
in complex ways but essentially as separate, distinct, and out of
relation.

The photographs on the jacket only frustrate any attempt to separate Duras from her speaker. The essential emptiness of these images is produced by the sense that identity can never be understood
in the ways we are accustomed to assuming we understand it.
Therefore, and strange to say, the photographs suggest instead the
impossibility of reproducing identity in representation. This impossibility is argued by the text itself with a passage describing not the
jacket photographs but a photograph of the speaker's mother. Except for the references to age, it might well describe the front jacket
photograph of Duras, which is itself minimal and almost featureless
and thus seems to have been constructed according to the same
conventions:

> All these photographs of different people, and I've seen many of
> them, gave practically identical results, the resemblance was

stunning. It wasn't because all old people look alike, but because the portraits themselves were invariably touched up in
such a way that any facial peculiarities, if there were any left,
were minimized. All the faces were prepared in the same way to
confront eternity, all toned down, all uniformly rejuvenated.
This is what people wanted. (96–97)

These images, records of individual subjects that will survive them,
leave only traces of those subjects. The individual is eclipsed, at first
by the fact of the representation and then by the effects produced
by the subversion of representation in the text.

Duras's text is fundamentally about crossing boundaries, decep-
tions, and displacements. It is the image of her crossing the Mekong
River that proves so compelling to the speaker in the present. The
image lasts the entire crossing, while the river suggests an unstable
region unstructured by the family or social inscriptions of desire,
sexuality, pleasure, and pain. It is only in this unstable terrain, this
interstice, that the speaker finds an image of herself she can recognize as somehow true to her memory: "I often think of the image
only I can see now, and of which I've never spoken. It's always
there, in the same silence, amazing. It's the only image of myself I
like, the only one in which I recognize myself, in which I delight"
(3–4). To cross the river, to separate oneself from family and community, to move from the known to the unknown, provides an escape only while one is moving. It is not, finally, to escape structuring powers—one brings the known into the unknown. Structures
are not easily escaped, and, even more, as the speaker suggests, one
does not necessarily want to escape them entirely.

Both the beggar woman and a figure upon whom the character
Anne-Marie Stretter seems to be based appear in *The Lover*, further
complicating relationships among writing, representation, and experience. The obscure reference to an unnamed Anne-Marie Stretter figure in *The Lover* resonates with what we know about Anne-
Marie Stretter from *The Vice-Consul* and *India Song*:

The Lady, they called her. She came from Savanna Khet. Her
husband was posted to Vinh Long. Because of the young man,
the assistant administrator in Savanna Khet. They couldn't be
lovers any more. So he shot himself. The story reached the new
posting in Vinh Long. The day she left Savanna Khet for Vinh

Long, a bullet through the heart. In the main square in broad daylight. Because of her young daughters and her husband's being posted to Vinh Long she'd told him it had to stop. (89)

That Anne-Marie Stretter, as well as the beggar woman of Calcutta, should appear, though unnamed, in *The Lover* establishes a connection between it and the Lol V. Stein cycle. In a curious way, this connection makes the Lol V. Stein cycle part of the autobiographical claims of *The Lover*, that paradoxical other space where autobiography and fiction merge, while it makes *The Lover* seem more fictional than autobiographical. That Duras has spoken in an interview of an Anne-Marie Stretter figure in her own life suggests her representations are inspired by an experience which itself disrupted boundaries:

With the very established, very visible colonial ostentation that surrounded me, this power of woman was not apparent: it was unexpected, it exploded just like that, like a bomb, but silently, you see. This accident wasn't ascribable to anything, nor could it be classified; it was natural, it had the fantastic violence of nature. It was either the cars of the rich or the cars of the poor, the children of the rich or the children of the poor, everything was like that, classified, codified, very clearly. And all of a sudden there was this accident that had nothing to do with the kind of arrangement of white social life in the posts. I think this is what struck me. It overwhelmed me. ("Dispossessed" 80)

This "accident" is a suicide: a young man apparently killed himself for a woman. Whether or not the story Duras heard as a child was true, it continued to haunt her. And this event is strikingly similar to the one she describes in *The Lover* where a young man kills himself for a woman who may have been called Stretter. Although Duras was only seven years old when this incident occurred, it had the tremendous impact of exploding her sense of the normal, conventional structure of colonial life. Because it occurred so many years ago when she was very young, it has the fictional aspect that memories acquire. It exists as a mythical moment, one outside normal experience, which nevertheless structures or influences the way subsequent events are conceptualized.

In *The Vice-Consul* the beggar woman abandons her children as she travels toward Calcutta. (At least in Peter Morgan's version, which draws on a story he has heard about a different beggar woman from Anne-Marie Stretter.) The beggar woman of *The Vice-Consul* also appears in *The Lover*, interwoven with the speaker's memories of her own mother in ways that suggest she felt as abandoned by her mother as the young man probably felt when forsaken by the woman who may have been called Stretter. What's interesting is that Duras adopts the story she had Peter Morgan write in the earlier text: what Duras's readers first encounter as a fiction—and not just fiction but writing that asserts power—seems to solidify into reality. In *The Vice-Consul*, Peter continues a story that Anne-Marie Stretter happens to mention; in *The Lover* the speaker builds upon Morgan's narrative. She claims to have encountered the beggar woman herself. But her two descriptions of the beggar woman are separated by a fragment in which she remembers her mother, all of which revolve around fear, identity, and madness. The juxtaposition suggests connections between the mother and this beggar woman who abandoned her children. The fear the speaker has of the beggar woman is articulated in the first description, which focuses on a childhood incident when the woman chased her at night. Afraid that to be touched by this woman is to become like her, the speaker flees, refusing the contact. In the second description, we read of the beggar woman's walk to Calcutta, a loose repetition of Morgan's story.

It is curious that along with these two descriptions, perhaps fictional, is an account of something that seems vivid and real. It is as if Duras uses the speaker, who in turn uses the beggar woman, to approach a subject too painful to tackle directly, without such a buffer. She describes her fear of seeing her mother in a certain state of mind. After refusing to name this state she continues:

> There, suddenly, close to me, was someone sitting in my mother's place who wasn't my mother, who looked like her but who had never been her. . . . My terror . . . came from the fact that she was sitting just where my mother had been sitting when the substitution took place, from the fact that I knew no one else was there in her place, but that that identity irreplaceable by any other had disappeared and I was powerless to make it come back, make it start to come back. There was no longer anything there to inhabit her image. I went mad in full possession of my senses. (85–86)

The speaker's experience of madness is quite different from the beggar woman's, for the latter seems beyond the capacity to be aware of her own misery. But like the speaker, who feels mad with betrayal and abandonment, the beggar woman is ostracized by family and community, rejected and abandoned by her mother for her illicit pregnancy. She is shunned for the violation of a social code, a transgression for which she pays dearly.

If the speaker is unable to speak directly of her own feelings of being abandoned, she nevertheless seems to displace a psychologically equivalent story onto the beggar woman. In the story of the beggar woman that circulates among these texts, after carrying her child 2,000 kilometers the beggar woman gives the girl away to a white stranger. Here a substitution takes place that is similar to the one she describes when watching her mother. At the same time she justifies her mother's behavior and suggests that her own need for a mother is not the only story that might get told, as if to tell her story without such a qualification would be to betray her mother in some unforgivable way. As Peter Morgan reconstructs the story of this beggar woman in *India Song*, she is devoured by the child she carries inside as she traverses the countryside in search of food. Her desire for food and for her own mother overwhelm her. When she finally eats a fish, she awakens in the middle of the night only to find that she is still hungry—the child has taken this from her as well.[19]

Instead of bringing writing and experience into alignment, this admittedly most autobiographical text insists on the gulf between them in ways both overt and submerged. The displacement of emotion from the mother to the figure of the beggar woman problematizes the gap and does not necessarily reduce it, for the status of the incident with the mother is, of course, open to question too. With such displacements and diversions, the text shapes a collage of fragmentary memories and reflections that proceed not according to the logic of space and time but rather according to some associative logic known only to the speaker. It is a logic based on forgetting, displacing, and substituting. It is not linear, for as the speaker claims, "The story of my life doesn't exist. Does not exist. There's never any center to it. No path, no line" (8). Despite this, however, the speaker does set about the task of representing something about her life: "I've written a good deal about the members of my family, but then they were alive, my mother and my brothers. And I skirted around them, skirted around all these things without really tackling them" (7). The implication is that now that the family is dead these things can be written about more directly. Now she will tackle difficult subjects; now she can be honest. And yet, since the identities of the speaker and those who surround her are constantly called into question, any quest for truth is deflected, any question of finding out the truth absurd.

In addition to all the other identities thrown into question, finally it isn't entirely clear, as Barbara Probst Solomon has noted, who the lover is. Most obviously, of course, it's the older Chinese man. But the younger brother is perhaps the most beloved. This leads Solomon to speculate whether *The Lover* might not be "a tale of incest designed to shock as miscegenation" (418). Solomon suggests that, if read as a story of incest, the text hides the shameful necessity for absolute silence about the true violation by substituting the Chinese lover for the brother. In this way, too, the speaker transfers guilt from herself to the Chinese man, though as Solomon points out, it makes more sense to think that the girl orchestrates the scene of seduction herself.[20] I'm not interested in trying to establish, especially on the questionable basis of *The Lover*, whether Duras did in fact have an incestuous experience with her brother. (Solomon, however, does speculate that Duras's "shameful incestuous affair with her brother . . . gets hidden and becomes obsessively and repetitively displaced by political images throughout her work, not as a device—but because it actually happened in that sequence" [419].) What is more important here in Solomon's argument is its relevance to seeing the associative structure of *The Lover* and its political digressions as a solution to the problem of representing what is simply too transgressive or shameful to represent. This brings us full circle, back to Woolf's internalized boundaries and fears of writing beyond sanctioned subjects and back to Barnes's strategies for telling and not telling. Duras's writing, in addition to subverting its own authority, functions, like Woolf's and like Barnes's, as a coded articulation of the forbidden. Like Woolf and Barnes, Duras both reveals and conceals.

The central contradiction in Duras's work resides in her ability to subvert established modes of representation on the one hand and the problems this subversion and its commitment to nonpositionality raise—particularly for feminists interested in changing material and discursive practices—on the other. Duras questions the ability of language to master or control its subjects. She challenges in a very self-conscious way the authority of the symbolic and its repression of what is unstructured, uncontrollable, and chaotic—in short, of what is, within the terms of the symbolic, equated with femininity. But what this subversion means for female subjects engaged in material practices is problematic. Duras's work enables us to question the connections between femininity as a product of discourse and the experience of women in the world. It enables us to examine the extent to which this discursive equation contributes to the marginality of women. And it enables us to see how identity is constituted by discourses and signifiers dismantled by the real, by what exceeds representation. But it also represents female subjects as necessarily marginal and chaotic within discourse, language, and culture. For these reasons, Duras's writing at once subverts and reinforces conventional notions of what it means to be female.

Afterword

The three women writers who have shaped this study represent in their fiction female experiences of being at once within and without representation and ideology. Woolf, Barnes, and Duras give literary form to female experiences of being produced by culture while they demonstrate how female subjects exceed these cultural constructions of femininity and normative ideas of what it means to be female. We are not, all three insist, equivalent to the cultural representations and definitions that nevertheless do shape us. We both are and are not women as they are defined and constructed in a patriarchal society. All three ask provocative questions about the contradictory nature of subjectivity and experience and provide contexts in which we can investigate both resistance and complicity. For to read these authors in the context of one another is to be in a position to examine ways in which resistance can blend almost imperceptively with complicity. It is to be able to see that resistance is rarely pure—and that it need not be in order to be effective. And furthermore, as Teresa De Lauretis has suggested, the extent to which our *awareness* of complicity enables female resistance or works against it is one of the important problems for feminist theory in the late twentieth century.

The condition of being outside or without ideology is, of course, theoretically problematic. If subjects are produced and constructed by particular cultural ideologies, how then is it possible to occupy positions outside that system of production and representation, positions from which the system can be analyzed and critiqued? Traditional Marxism and structuralist social theory are unable to account fully for such a process. But recent poststructuralist theory is perhaps more useful because it maintains that no system, social or linguistic, can ever hope to be completely self-contained or authoritative: given the very nature of symbolic structures and systems, no system can ever attain a direct equivalence with lived experience. There will always be a gap between discourse and experience. Moreover, systems are composed of shifting contradictory elements and gaps—and in these mutable parts and spaces there exists the possibility for movement and change, for finding positions not completely contained and controlled by a given discursive structure.

Much late-twentieth-century feminist literary criticism has shown how women writers resist an oppressive status quo from positions outside the official ideology—that is, it focuses on the ways women writers have extended the positions available to us outside ideology by representing or producing female experiences that differ from or openly contradict the official stories the normalizing and dominant culture tells about female experience. This focus is hardly surprising, for feminism's goals are rooted in a commitment to social change, and thus it is in feminism's best interest to resist and subvert. Not only because they are women writers but because their writing represents such experiences from perspectives that are to some extent outside ideology, Woolf, Barnes, and Duras are subversive writers.

In contrast to the condition of being without ideology, the condition of being within it is not as theoretically problematic. But it remains problematic for feminists, who have strong reasons for working hard to position themselves outside ideology. To be within ideology is to be produced by social structures inherently oppressive to women—and to be produced by such structures is to be constructed as subjects who will participate in the activity of reproducing existing social conditions. And though Woolf, Barnes, and Duras critique, subvert, and resist oppressive social structures, they also represent and demonstrate some of the ways in which women reproduce and thus remain complicit with those structures.

Because these writers resist conventional, normalizing ideologies but do not attempt to step completely outside existing structures into utopian, imaginary, female worlds, their texts are essentially ambivalent and contradictory. And this doubleness, these structures, which both assert and undermine, resist and reinforce, cannot be understood fully within the context of deconstruction, which asserts that, given its very nature, writing always undermines itself and is fundamentally contradictory. What this perspective leaves out is the importance of gender and experience. The ambivalence and contradiction in the work of Woolf, Barnes, and Duras have everything to do with female experiences—and perhaps especially with experiences of vulnerability and powerlessness—in the world. The impulse in the fiction to both reveal and conceal can be traced to this experience of vulnerability.

To recognize when and why women participate in the reproduction of existing structures that oppress us is an essential feminist project. Such recognition makes us aware of ourselves in more complex ways—in ways that are not purified or distilled—and awareness need not lead to resignation or despair. It should instead enable new forms of female resistance.

Notes

1 Introduction

1. Defining twentieth-century modernisms is fraught with difficulty, given the diversity of new forms and techniques that developed in this period. However, most descriptions emphasize breaks with previous literary forms and techniques, historical discontinuities, rejection of traditional values, and crises in representation. For instance, Bradbury and McFarlane suggest that the high canonical modernism that took shape in the early part of the century was an extraordinary compound of oppositions and includes both revolutionary and conservative impulses: "It was a celebration of the technological age and a condemnation of it; an excited acceptance of the belief that the old regimes of culture were over, and a deep despairing in the face of that fear; a mixture of convictions that the new forms were escapes from historicism and the pressures of the time with convictions that they were precisely the living expressions of these things" (46).

2. Feminist critics working on gender and twentieth-century modernisms tend to focus their efforts in two distinct areas. The first group, like DeKoven, rereads literary texts through the work of female writers and shows how the inclusion of women writers requires a reconsideration of traditional conceptualizations. Shari Benstock, Rachel Blau DuPlessis, Sandra Gilbert, Susan Gubar, Jane Marcus, and Elaine Showalter have made significant contributions to this effort. In *No Man's Land*, Gilbert and Gubar argue that modernism is differently inflected for male and female writers. According to Gilbert and Gubar, by emphasizing the "despair in the face of the new," traditional definitions of modernism fail to point out the tremendous opportunities the twentieth century afforded women writers: if female modernists shared in a pervasive cultural despair, their relationship to this despair is contradictory because at the same time women were

enjoying more freedom. Analyses of gender and representations of gender force us to reconsider the shapes and purposes of modernist writing.

If for this first group of critics the important difference is between male and female writers, for the second it is a difference *within* biological sexed beings—or in texts. From this perspective, it is, theoretically, possible for a male writer to write "as a woman." It is not difference but the Derridean notion of *différance* that interests these theorists, a group which includes, among others, Jane Gallop, Alice Jardine, and Toril Moi. Analyses of male-authored texts, such as Jardine undertakes in *Gynesis* or Gallop in *The Daughter's Seduction*, show how the "feminine" in language has been historically repressed and reasserts itself in literature, especially literature of the twentieth century.

3. In "A Sketch of the Past," Woolf recalls how, when she was very small, her half brother Gerald Duckworth lifted her onto a ledge outside the dining room door and explored her body. Later, when she was about twenty, her other half brother, George Duckworth, began making advances which seemed to her distinctly sexual. While, as Phyllis Rose points out, Woolf "never accused him of anything more than ambiguously erotic gestures, never that is, accused him of actually raping her, she regarded his behavior as sexually criminal and called him (with relish) her 'seducing half-brother' " (8). In "22 Hyde Park Gate," which Woolf read to the Memoir Club composed of the Bloomsbury group, George flings himself on her in bed one evening after a particularly provocative evening at the theater. She comments, "Yes, the old ladies of Kensington and Belgravia never knew that George Duckworth was not only father and mother, brother and sister to those poor Stephen girls; he was their lover also" (177). In *Virginia Woolf: The Impact of Childhood Sexual Abuse on Her Life and Work*, Louise DeSalvo argues that Woolf's biographers have underplayed these incidents. Using recent work on childhood sexual abuse, DeSalvo reads Woolf's life and her fiction as intimately connected to these and other early traumatic events. In addition, as Mitchell Leaska's *Pointz Hall*, which contains the early typescripts of *Between the Acts*, shows, Woolf eliminated some passages suggesting the incestuous relationship between Bart Oliver and his sister Lucy Swithin as she revised the manuscript, making that relationship even more indirectly represented.

4. *Nightwood* is not the only Barnes text to deal with incest. In *The Antiphon*, the mother allows the father to seduce the daughter. Andrew Field claims that Barnes "was not exactly seduced or raped but rather 'given' sexually by her father like an Old Testament slave or daughter" to one of his friends (43). Field also notes that "evidence of the molestation by collusion is in the art, in the original manuscript of *Nightwood* that Barnes acknowledged in a letter to T. S. Eliot was to be regarded as a semi-autobio-

graphical story. . . . In the unpublished manuscript portion the girl . . . [who would become Nora] is initiated by an older man who had held her on his knee when she was a child and ate caramels and melted because she looked up at him and said, 'Yes,' and then he was frightened because she would not cry afterwards. . . . [Later] the girl loses her virginity yet again, this time to her father" (43). As in *The Antiphon*, in the draft the mother sprinkles flour outside the girl's door to check for footprints, but she does not intervene or protect the girl.

5. Barbara Solomon points out that Duras recently has spoken explicitly about the role of incest in her work and suggests that the forbidden Chinese lover in *The Lover* might mask an even more illicit intimacy between the speaker and the younger brother.

6. For an elaboration of these ideas see Teresa De Lauretis, *Alice Doesn't* and *Technologies of Gender*.

7. Woolf, Barnes, and Duras write fiction that is distinctive for its lyricism. While lyrical writing seems different from other fiction, in the broadest sense the lyrical novel is an arbitrary concept, for most prose fiction contains lyrical passages, and all writing is in some sense rhythmic. In *The Lyrical Novel*, Ralph Freedman recognizes the problem implicit in defining just what constitutes a "lyrical novel" and refuses to define such novels by their prosodic features alone. Instead he argues that lyrical novels are not just novels with more lyrical passages than we are accustomed to but rather novels that attempt to reconcile antithetical impulses. He suggests that such novels combine narrative (which moves linearly through time and space) with lyricism (which absorbs action into an instantaneous revelation or illumination).

Like Freedman, I think the lyrical novel expresses a distinctly twentieth-century approach to experience, one that focuses in new ways on subjective perception and registers ambivalence through antithetical impulses. It is possible, therefore, to argue that lyrical fiction registers ambivalence and contradiction through its very forms. But my analysis of lyrical texts by Woolf, Barnes, and Duras differs from Freedman's study in several ways. Though I agree that lyrical prose puts antithetical impulses into play, the texts I examine here do not resolve or reconcile such oppositions. And I am less interested in isolating the strictly formal features of lyrical fiction than in analyzing how women writers use lyrical prose to articulate antithetical—that is, ambivalent and contradictory—aspects of female subjectivity and experience. Although Woolf's writing is central to Freedman's study, he is not interested in how or whether gender affects her lyricism. By shifting the focus to gender I want to argue not that there is a gender-specific use of lyricism but that these writers develop lyrical prose in order to represent experiences particular to women. With such writing they point toward the difficulty of giving any form at all to certain aspects of experience, whether owing to the nature and limitations of language or to social conditions mandating silence.

8. See Roland Barthes, *Mythologies* and *S/Z*.

9. DuPlessis argues that when a significantly large group of the populace begins to feel outside these plots, individual authors are able to break the sequence of conventional plot structures.

10. Kristeva's semiotic originates with the preverbal body, that is, with those drives and energies not already inscribed by language and culture. To foreground language's rhythmic properties is not, however, to regress to some earlier stage of development. It is rather a strategy to emphasize the noncoincidence between language as a symbolic structure and the subject's experience as a partially uninscribed entity in the world. That is to say, to write the body in this way is to assert that the body always exceeds language and symbolization. It is to question the status of representation. It is an especially powerful way for women writers concerned with the ways culture contains and purifies female subjectivity to resist dominant discourses.

11. Kristeva is interested in the conditions that might make this poetic practice correspond to socioeconomic change and revolution or, alternatively, merely a "blind alley, a harmless bonus offered by a social order which uses [it] to expand, become flexible, and thrive" (16). But she never satisfactorily identifies just what these conditions might be, and examples are hard to find. In fact, her attempt to link language and social revolution has been widely criticized, since whatever links might exist between language and experience are not necessarily causal.

12. Current postmodern theory also accounts for contradiction, ambivalence, and open-endedness in both form and content. It shows how, in the work of both male and female writers, these strategies denaturalize our experience by making us aware of how what we experience as "natural" is in fact "cultural." See Hal Foster, *The Anti-Aesthetic* and *Recodings: Art, Spectacle, Cultural Politics*; Linda Hutcheon, *The Politics of Postmodernism*; and Brian Wallis, ed., *Art after Modernism: Rethinking Representation*. Because feminist theory denaturalizes gender and sexuality, it shares certain features with postmodernism. But feminism is committed to social change, whereas not all forms of postmodernism are. And it is very much concerned with the material conditions of women in the world. Combinations of feminism and postmodernism, as in the work of the female writers I discuss in this study, are therefore very different from the work of male writers who also produce representations that are ambivalent, contradictory, and open-ended. My point is not that men do not produce such representations but that women's experiences in the world and the commitment

of feminists to social change complicate their representations of ambivalence and contradiction.

2   The Lyrical Body in Virginia Woolf's Fiction

1. Adrienne Rich is of particular interest here because of the way she
combines art and politics. As her work becomes political in a more general
and less subjective way, it also becomes less lyrical, suggesting that the
lyrical mode is less suited to explicit political commentary or polemical
stances.

2. In addition to Elaine Showalter and Jane Marcus, around whom feminist criticism of Woolf's work has developed, there are numerous articles
published in the last decade from feminist perspectives (see notes 4 and
16). Also, Phyllis Rose and Lyndall Gordon have provided alternative biog-
raphies focusing on Woolf's feminism, while Louise DeSalvo's work, which
looks at Woolf as an incest victim and survivor, departs from the other bi-
ographies in fundamental ways.

3. Marcus sees Woolf's position as more limited than I believe it is. For
Marcus, Woolf's insistence that art and politics be kept distinct is a response to the political art of the 1930s, not to art more generally. While this
is to some extent true, Woolf's conviction seems to extend beyond that precise moment.

4. Madeline Moore extends Showalter's position by arguing that Woolf
withdrew from the world by "retreating into ever more impersonal states of
mysticism" (16). Mystical renunciation and illness become preludes to
creativity. As Woolf writes: "I believe these illnesses are in my case—how
shall I express it—partly mystical. Something happens in my mind. It becomes chrysalis. I lie quite torpid, often with acute physical pain. . . . Then
suddenly something springs" (*A Writer's Diary* 150). Moore analyzes
Woolf's asceticism in terms of her choice to be asexual with both men and
women and her tendency toward anorexia nervosa.

Makiko Minow-Pinkney and Pamela Transue have argued for more radical readings of Woolf's style. Minow-Pinkney reads the novels from a poststructuralist perspective, focusing on the instability of the subject and
meaning. Transue addresses the ways Woolf's art embodies feminist and
political polemics, though perhaps not as radically as some might wish.

5. In *Virginia Woolf and the Real World*, Alex Zwerdling studies Woolf's
social vision in relation to her fiction. This is one of the best studies of Woolf
because he addresses the complexities and contradictions in her work more
fully than most.

6. Given the influence of French feminism and critical theory as well as
a more general and certainly more explicit twentieth-century interest in the

body and sexuality—what Foucault has called the "discourse of sexuality"—it is very likely that the obstacles to writing the body are complex for both male and female writers. If language and discourse always mediate a subject's perception of the real, we can never know the real in any unmediated way, only through its formulation in discourse and representation. Therefore the body is to a great extent inaccessible, though as Kristeva suggests, in another sense it is always present in language. For Kristeva, rhythm, repetition, and cadence in language originate with the body and are structured according to principles different from the symbolic properties that actually produce meaning.

7. DeSalvo's book is valuable for its revisionist perspective, but, even though I am sympathetic to her project, it is still difficult to determine just what happened with George. DeSalvo's interpretation of events occasionally seems quite speculative, given the evidence in the *Letters* and *Diaries*.

8. Woolf does allude to the incident in earlier letters to Ethel Smyth.

9. While this selection leaves out other important novels, such as *Mrs. Dalloway*, I don't mean that ambivalence is less operative in those texts. In *Mrs. Dalloway*, for instance, Woolf is ambivalent about Mrs. Dalloway herself. At times sympathetic with her, Woolf also seems quite critical of Mrs. Dalloway and her limitations.

10. For an extended analysis of the relevance of Chodorow's work to Woolf's fiction and the subject of mothers and daughters in the novels see Ellen Roseman, *The Invisible Presence*. For a similar discussion from a postmodern perspective see Patricia Waugh, *Feminine Fictions*.

11. Gayatri Spivak makes a similar claim in "Unmaking and Making in *To the Lighthouse*," an essay in which she puts the text to use in demonstrating Derridean deconstruction.

12. Makiko Minow-Pinkney's *Virginia Woolf and the Problem of the Subject* is the first extended study to use Kristeva to analyze Woolf's writing of the feminine. Minow-Pinkney finds in Woolf's notion of androgyny "the principle of difference, not the logic of identity" (8). She examines the convergence between feminism and modernism in Lacanian terms: modernism reintroduces the repressed imaginary, whereas what is sometimes referred to as a feminine discourse challenges the fixity of identity and gender.

13. For Kristeva, deconstruction exemplifies this pretense of giving up power: the subject "sets himself up with even more power in this situation inasmuch as he will mime the dissolution of all positions" (*Revolution* 97).

14. In "O'Keeffe and the Masculine Gaze," Anna C. Chave makes a similar argument about Georgia O'Keeffe's work. Chave notes that O'Keeffe's work has been eroticized from a male perspective but argues that it offers a "woman's often vivid, poetic and evocative visual report on her own experience of her body and her desires" (116). She adds that "since women

have not been constituted as subjects under patriarchy, they have had no legitimate basis for experiencing, let alone describing, their own desire. . . . And insofar as her art endeavored to position itself outside the existing visual practice in which 'woman is constituted as the ground of representation . . . it was, in a sense, both subversive and hygienic'" (124).

15. Of course, almost all spoken and written language has some kind of rhythm or pattern of sound, however irregular it might be. It is an inherent quality of language. In poetry, rhythm is sometimes tightly controlled. In prose, rhythm is generally produced merely in the course of using language to make a point, though it can also be used to achieve a certain effect. For instance, in sentences, parallel structures repeat patterns, perhaps with some variation, depending on the effect one desires. Stretched to an extreme, such balance produces the sense that things fall into place. My intent, however, is not to work out a definition of rhythm or to use it in a specialized way. Instead, I want to suggest that in *The Waves*, Woolf uses rhythm not as a rhetorical device but as a means of fracturing rhetoric. Instead of enhancing the significance of a sentence, Woolf's strategy of "writing to a rhythm" introduces an impulse capable of dismantling rhetorical structures in language that produce meaning.

16. See Jane Marcus, "Liberty, Sorority, Misogyny"; Madeline Moore, *The Short Season between Two Silences*; Eileen Barrett, "Matriarchal Myth on a Patriarchal Stage: Virginia Woolf's *Between the Acts*"; Nora Eisenberg, "Virginia Woolf's Last Words on Words: *Between the Acts* and 'Anon'"; Sallie Sears, "Theater of War: Virginia Woolf's *Between the Acts*"; and Judith Johnston, "The Remediable Flaw: Revisioning Cultural History in *Between the Acts*."

17. *New Larousse Encyclopedia of Mythology* 183.

18. See Ellen Barrett (note 16) and Judy Little, "Festive Comedy in Woolf's *Between the Acts*."

19. See also Evelyn Haller, "Isis Unveiled: Virginia Woolf's Use of Egyptian Myth."

3 Djuna Barnes and the Politics of the Night

1. Benstock's notes suggest she has drawn her own analysis from Jane Marcus's work with the original manuscripts, and she writes that Marcus's "preliminary findings suggest that Eliot was particularly uncomfortable with the connections Barnes drew between the expression of lesbian anger and societal institutions, particularly the church" (476n9).

2. The manuscripts for *Nightwood* are part of the Djuna Barnes collection in the Porter Room of McKeldin Library at the University of Maryland, College Park. There are various edited versions, which is perhaps why it is hard to separate changes Barnes initiated from changes initiated by Eliot.

Given the rejection of the manuscript by so many publishers, it no doubt must have seemed preferable to Barnes to have it published in a reduced, altered form than not published at all. The library also holds a collection of correspondence between Barnes and Eliot, some of which discusses changes made to *Nightwood* and which may help in sorting all this out.

3. Like many modernists, Barnes drew on her life in Paris to create the context and atmosphere of *Nightwood*. Although it can be reductive to read a literary text strictly in terms of its author's life, in addition to more recent critics, many of Barnes's contemporaries and even Thelma Wood herself apparently took Robin Vote as a portrayal of Thelma. One notable exception is Lynn DeVore, who demonstrates the similarity between the language Barnes used to describe Robin and her descriptions of her close friend Baroness Elsa Von-Freytag. In some cases the language is identical, which suggests at the very least that Robin is not just a portrait of Thelma.

4. The letters Barnes and Eliot exchanged over the years include discussions of Barnes's later work. One of the reasons Eliot's involvement elicits the desire to see the entire manuscript is his ambivalent attitude toward Barnes's work. He praised *Nightwood* but wrote mixed praise for the jacket of *The Antiphon*: "From the point of view of the conventionally minded *The Antiphon* would be still more shocking—or would be if they could understand it—and still more tedious—because they will not understand it—than *Nightwood*. It might be said of Miss Barnes, who is incontestably one of the most original writers of our time, that never has so much genius been combined with so little talent" (Field 222).

5. See the discussion of *Between the Acts* in the previous chapter for an extended treatment of this kind of postmodern textual erotics.

6. Before her expatriation, if she was not exactly politically active, Barnes's activities and journalistic writing indicate that she was politically aware. Field points out that in 1914 "she did some anti-war drawings for the Pacifist movement prior to America's entry into the First World War" (15). And during this period her journalistic writing and interviews of various people, are informed by strong personal and social views. In these interviews, even as she makes the personalities central and vivid, Barnes herself emerges as a distinctive presence (see Douglas Messerli's *Djuna Barnes Interviews*). Although she didn't follow her grandmother's lead and join the women's suffrage movement, Barnes's sympathy with the suffragists is suggested by her willingness in 1914 to undergo the kind of force-feeding that was then being inflicted on the English suffragists. She found it an "anguish beyond description" (Field 53):

If I, play acting, felt my being burning with revolt at this brutal usurpation of my own functions, how they who actually suffered the ordeal in its acutest horror must have flamed at the violation of the sanctuaries of their spirit? I saw in my hysteria a vision of a hundred women in grim prison hospitals, bound and shrouded on tables just like this, held in the rough grip of callous warders, while white-robed doctors thrust rubber tubing into the delicate interstices of their nostrils and forced into their helpless bodies the crude fuel to sustain the life they longed to sacrifice. (Field 54)

Barnes knew from this rather dramatic experience the demoralization of having her will and body blatantly overpowered and violated—albeit by her own consent—by official and "legitimate" custodians of social order and control. But despite this early political involvement, Barnes later claimed to be apolitical, a position she maintained "through the decades of depression, communism, fascism, war, and McCarthyism" (Field 15).

7. James Scott and Louis Kannenstine are two early critics who argue that *Ladies Almanack* is actually an attack on lesbian love.

8. Lanser writes that "this ending may seem lewdly patriarchal, in bad taste, irreverent, even grotesque; I confess to discomfort in reading it," but adds "this wild finale of *Ladies Almanack* surely celebrates, proclaims, the gift of tongues" (44). A revised version of Lanser's essay appears in *Silence and Power*. Although published too late to be of use here, the essays in *Silence and Power* promise to be influential in Barnes scholarship.

9. See Foucault's "The Discourse on Language" in *The Archeaology of Knowledge*.

10. See Hélène Cixous, "Castration or Decapitation" and "The Laugh of the Medusa."

11. For a more complete discussion of cross-dressing in *Nightwood* and in other modernist texts see Sandra Gilbert, "Costumes of the Mind: Transvestism as Metaphor in Modern Literature," and Susan Gubar, "Blessings in Disguise: Cross-Dressing as Re-Dressing for Female Modernists."

12. John Berger, *Ways of Seeing*.

13. In "Laughing at Leviticus," Marcus writes that "Robin is in fear because she is being written about. Nora experiences the dream as 'something being done to Robin, Robin disfigured and eternalized by the hieroglyphics of sleep and pain' (*N* 63)—that is, being made into La Somnambule. As publicist for the circus, Nora is dreaming herself into the male role of master of ceremonies, Djuna Barnes writing this novel as circus" (246).

4 Marguerite Duras and the Subversion of Power

1. See Mary Douglass, *Purity and Danger: An Analysis of Concepts of Pollution and Taboo*.

2. Drawing on the work of Deleuze and Guattari, Leo Bersani argues that the effects of a culture of repression and sublimation provide, in themselves, the reason for exploring the possibilities of desublimating desire: "Psychic coherence involves a serious crippling of desire. The viability of the structured self depends on an impoverishment of desire. The desiring imagination's contacts with the world are limited by the need for preserving the intelligibility of a psychic structure. Even more dangerously, the renunciation of desire, as Freud suggested, may increase our sense of guilt instead of assuaging it. And heightened guilt welcomes the potentially ferocious punishments of conscience and of external moral authority. An important psychological consequence of sublimated (civilized) desire may be suicidal melancholy. . . . the endless repetition of desires suppressed by guilt and angry frustration ultimately leads to the fantasy of death as the absolute pleasure" (6).

3. Winifred Woodhull writes that this text "exposes the political consequences of prevailing forms of symbolic exchange. The apparent accessibility of the media and the 'free speech' they seem to permit prove illusory or are rendered ineffective by the structure of consumption: individuals are organized by hierarchized relations such as the one between the narrator and Claire, and . . . have little in common but their isolation" (7). Woodhull traces this social fragmentation to the symbolic mediation of needs and desires, which, according to Jean Baudrillard, are governed by the logic of the commodity.

4. Willis explores this impasse with a discussion of Nancy K. Miller and Peggy Kamuf: "For Nancy Miller, it is necessary to maintain a concern for the status of the woman writing, in the interest of producing connections with the woman reading, with women in the world. . . . For Peggy Kamuf, however, to lay too much stress on the referent is to hypostatize a category of woman to place over against masculine discourse, and thereby to remain within its humanist boundaries" (13). See also note 2 to chapter 1.

5. Jacques Lacan, "Homage to Marguerite Duras" in *Marguerite Duras*.

6. This is how Duras describes her meeting with Lacan: "Lacan had me meet him one night in a bar at midnight. He frightened me. In a bar in a basement. To talk to me about *Lol V. Stein*. He told me that it was a *clinically perfect* delirium. He began to ask me questions. For two hours. I more or less staggered out of the place" ("An Interview with Marguerite Duras" 129). Duras's description of this meeting with Lacan raises questions about masculine forms of mastery, control, and appropriation. If Lacanian psychoanalysis describes (if not entirely supports) the process by which subjectivity is effected in language as sexist, because male-centered, the meeting as Duras describes it reveals concomitant social practices produced as the result of such male privilege.

7. My discussion of Lacan is very brief and focuses only on some aspects of his thought relevant to my discussion. For a more complete exposition, see Lacan's *Ecrits*. For helpful secondary discussions see Jane Gallop, *The Daughter's Seduction*, or the introductions by Jacqueline Rose and Juliet Mitchell to Lacan's thought in *Feminine Sexuality*.

8. Jardine mentions Michele Montrelay's *L'ombre et le nom* and Christiane Rabant's "La bête chanteuse." Jardine (173) explains that for Montrelay, Lol is "the figure of femininity—not the representation of a woman. She is . . . a figure of Lacan's Real: 'There remains to S. Thala of Lol: two night-bird eyes destroyed by the light, dead from having nothing left to see. An uninhabited body, deserted, fallen to the ground like a stone, reduced to its matter: the Real' (*L'ombre*, p. 18)." Jardine also points out that these writers do little more than echo Lacan's "Homage to Marguerite Duras."

9. Mary Lydon reads Lacan's remarks about Duras differently from Jardine: "What Lacan recognized in Duras' art was not, or not simply . . . that she 'understood his theory,' but that her writing was the artistic embodiment of the real scandal of psychoanalysis: that is, the unconscious and the splitting of the subject that its discovery implied. As Lacan has it: 'the abyss that opened up at the thought that a thought should make itself heard in the abyss'" (262).

10. Duras's textual practice is very much rooted in repetitions with slight variations. Compare the following pair of quotations:

> Lol V. Stein was born here, in S. Thala, and here she spent a good part of her youth. Her father was a professor at the university. She has a brother nine years older than she—I have never seen him—they say he lives in Paris. Her parents are dead. . . . Lol was nineteen when she met Michael Richardson playing tennis one morning during summer vacation. He was twenty-five. He was the only son of well-to-do parents, whose real estate holdings in the T. Beach area were considerable. He did no real work. Their parents consented to the marriage. Lol must have been engaged for six months, the wedding was to take place in the autumn, she had just finished her final year of school and was on vacation in T. Beach when the biggest ball of the season was held at the Municipal Casino. (*Ravissement* 11–12; my translation)

> Lol spent her entire youth here in S. Thala, her father was of German origin, he was a history professor at the University, her mother was from S. Thala, Lol has a brother nine years older than she, he lives in Paris, she never talks about him, Lol met the man from T. Beach one morning during summer vacation at the tennis courts, he was twenty-five years old, the only son of well-to-do parents who owned a

great deal of land in the area, without employment, cultured, brilliant, extremely brilliant, melancholy, Lol fell in love with him at first sight. (*Ravissement*, 102; my translation)

11. All translations of *L'Amour* are mine.

12. That this figure is in fact Michael Richardson is suggested more explicitly in the film *L'Amour*. Elisabeth Lyon writes that *L'Amour* "reopens the story of Lol V. Stein in S. Thala with the return of Michael Richardson many years later to the fantasmic scene of the ball. It is from this matrix of madness and fantasy that Duras later drew the film *La Femme du Gange*" (8). If the connection seems clear to film critics, however, it does not seem quite so obvious to Duras's literary critics, who generally treat *L'Amour* more abstractly, as does Sharon Willis in *Marguerite Duras: Writing on the Body*.

13. The heterosexual structuring of desire is unraveled in *India Song* and *Blue Eyes, Black Hair*, where it is also explicitly homoerotic. And if one reads, as I do, against Jacques Hold's structuring of desire in *The Ravishing of Lol Stein*, it is more heterogeneous there too.

14. In *Woman to Woman*, Duras explains her sense of the connections between the Vice-Consul and Anne-Marie Stretter: "There's an equivalence. It's more than an identification; there's an equivalence between Anne-Marie Stretter's pain and the French vice-consul's anger. It flows in her, you see, like a river that's traveled through her; it's as if she's tunneled by this river of pain, if you like, whereas he, by contrast . . . is like an engine of . . . well, of death; he's full of fire, and explosives, finally . . . all that has to get out, burst; it has to get expressed on the outside, be public, loud, whereas the entry . . . Anne-Marie Stretter's entry within India is . . . is carnal. It's internal" (127).

15. The connections Duras sometimes makes between violence and sexuality can be profoundly disturbing. Mary Lydon, in her article about translating this Duras story, writes: "For the anglophone reader with a feminist consciousness, whose aspirations might include a vision of a happy nonviolent sexual union . . . 'L'Homme assis dans le couloir' in particular may be hard to swallow" (261). This story, even more than Duras's other texts, links violence, pain, and pleasure with sexuality, gender, and desire.

16. "Notes on Voices 1 and 2" in *India Song*, 9–10.

17. William F. Van Wert, in an essay where he also discusses his experience teaching Duras's films, writes that "what makes *India Song* such a masterful film is Duras's complex and innovative use of sound. The two voices of *Woman of the Ganges* return for the first half of *India Song*, but are gradually succeeded by two other voices, one of which (a male voice) is fascinated by the fiction at hand and asks the other (the voice of Duras) to

help him remember, and her voice, while providing the details, also fears for the safety of the 'partner' voice. . . . these voices are anonymous and the characters within the frame are supposedly unaware of them. For example, Michael Richardson fondles the partially naked body of Anne-Marie Stretter. Duras's notation for the scene is as follows: 'The hand of Michael Richardson—the lover—stops at precisely that moment (the moment when the second voice declares: "I love you with an absolute desire"), as though this last phrase of the second voice caused him to stop.' Conversely, these women's voices slow down and follow the rhythm of the lover's hand, and their monotone breaks into a lyrical chant" (28).

18. Duras has said that many readers, both male and female, have written to her and said, "Reading your books has made me sick" (*Woman to Woman* 6).

19. In *The Daughter's Seduction*, Jane Gallop criticizes Luce Irigaray for speaking in such writings as "When Our Lips Speak Together" entirely from the daughter's position in relation to the mother. By doing so, Gallop argues, Irigaray makes the mother into a phallic mother, an all-powerful figure upon whom the daughter might depend. The problem with this is that it eclipses the mother's position as a human subject. In contrast, Gallop invokes Julia Kristeva, for Kristeva offers a different perspective in that she at least tries to speak from the mother's position as well. To speak in this way is to explode the myth of the phallic mother, to expose the vulnerability of the mother—who is herself a daughter. The mother exists much as woman does—as a cultural icon upon which we project our needs, fears, blame, and inadequacies. But we do so unfairly, for it is ultimately an empty space. By speaking from the mother's place with the beggar woman, Duras achieves something similar to Kristeva's exposure of the masquerade of the phallic mother.

20. Solomon writes that "the sexual exotic, really is the French girl, not the man. In the important first seduction scene she is in control. The fifteen-year-old narrator commands the horrified man to seduce her: 'Treat me like you treat the other woman.' But would a Chinese millionaire's son, who had lived in Paris and known many French women, be weeping and what I call mewling like a stuck pig at the thought of making love to a sexy French girl he had picked up?" She continues by asking: "And why would an adolescent affair with an adoring Chinese man who promises to—and apparently does—love the girl forever permanently ravage and ruin the young girl's face? *What* is the tragedy?" (419).

Bibliography

I list here only those writings that have been of use in the making of this book. This bibliography is by no means a complete record of all the works and sources I have consulted.

Albright, Daniel. *Lyricality in English Literature*. Lincoln: University of Nebraska Press, 1985.

Althusser, Louis. "Ideology and Ideological State Apparatuses." In *Lenin and Philosophy*. New York: Monthly Review Press, 1971.

Arnold, Matthew. *The Poems of Matthew Arnold*. Ed. Kenneth Allott. New York: Longman, 1965.

Barnes, Djuna. *The Antiphon*. London: Faber and Faber, 1958.

———. *Ladies Almanack*. New York: Harper and Row, 1972. Privately printed Robert McAlmon, 1928.

———. *Nightwood*. London: Faber and Faber, 1936. New York: Harcourt, Brace, 1937.

Barrett, Eileen. "Matriarchal Myth on a Patriarchal Stage: Virginia Woolf's *Between the Acts*." *Twentieth Century Literature* 33 (Spring 1987): 18–37.

Barthes, Roland. *Mythologies*. Trans. Annette Lavers. New York: Hill and Wang, 1972. Paris: Editions du Seuil, 1957.

———. *The Pleasure of the Text*. Trans. Richard Miller. New York: Hill and Wang, 1984. Originally published as *Le plaisir du texte*. Paris: Editions du Seuil, 1973.

———. *S/Z*. Trans. Richard Miller. New York: Hill and Wang, 1972. Paris: Editions du Seuil, 1970.

Baudrillard, Jean. *For a Critique of the Political Economy of the Sign*. Trans. Charles Levin. St. Louis: Telos Press, 1981. Originally published as *Pour une critique de l'économie politique du signe*. Paris: Editions Gallimard, 1972.

Benstock, Shari. *Women of the Left Bank: Paris, 1900–1940*. Austin: University of Texas Press, 1986.

Berger, John. *Ways of Seeing*. New York: Viking Press, 1973.

Bersani, Leo. *A Future for Astynax: Character and Desire in Literature*. Boston: Little, Brown and Company, 1976.

Bradbury, Malcolm, and James McFarlane. "The Name and Nature of Modernism." In *Modernism*. Ed. Malcolm Bradbury and James McFarlane. New York: Penguin, 1976.

Broe, Mary Lynn. "My Art Belongs to Daddy." In *Women's Writing in Exile*. Ed. Mary Lynn Broe and Angela Ingram. Chapel Hill: University of North Carolina Press, 1989.

———, ed. *Silence and Power: Djuna Barnes: A Reevaluation*. Carbondale: Southern Illinois University Press, 1991.

Brontë, Emily. *Wuthering Heights*. London: Penguin, 1965.

Brownstein, Marilyn L. "Postmodern Language and the Perpetuation of Desire." *Twentieth Century Literature* 31 (Spring 1985): 73–88.

Chave, Anna C. "O'Keeffe and the Masculine Gaze." *Art in America* (January 1990): 115–124.

Chodorow, Nancy. "Mothering, Object-Relations, and the Female Oedipal Configuration." *Feminist Studies* 4 (1978): 137–158.

———. *The Reproduction of Mothering: Psychoanalysis and the Sociology of Gender*. Berkeley: University of California Press, 1978.

Cixous, Hélène. "Castration or Decapitation?" Trans. Annette Kuhn. *Signs* 7 (1981): 41–55.

———. "The Laugh of the Medusa." Trans. Keith Cohen and Paula Cohen. *Signs* 2 (1976): 39–54.

Conrad, Joseph. *Heart of Darkness*. New York: Norton, 1987.

DeKoven, Marianne. "Gendered Doubleness and the 'Origins' of Modernist Form." *Tulsa Studies in Women's Literature* 8 (1989): 19–42.

De Lauretis, Teresa. *Alice Doesn't: Feminism, Semiotics, Cinema*. Bloomington: Indiana University Press, 1984.

———. *Technologies of Gender*. Bloomington: Indiana University Press, 1987.

Deleuze, Gilles, and Felix Guattari. *Anti-Oedipus: Capitalism and Schizophrenia*. Trans. Robert Hurley, Mark Seem, and Helen R. Lane. Minneapolis: University of Minnesota Press, 1983. Originally published as *L'Anti-Oedipe*. Paris: Minuit, 1972.

DeSalvo, Louise. *Virginia Woolf: The Impact of Childhood Sexual Abuse on Her Life and Work*. Boston: Beacon, 1989.

DeVore, Lynn. "The Backgrounds of *Nightwood*: Robin, Felix, and Nora." *Journal of Modern Literature* 10 (1983): 71–90.

Douglass, Mary. *Purity and Danger: An Analysis of Concepts of Pollution and Taboo*. New York: Praeger, 1966.

DuPlessis, Rachel Blau. *Writing beyond the Ending: Narrative Strategies of Twentieth-Century Women Writers*. Bloomington: Indiana University Press, 1985.

Duras, Marguerite. *L'Amante Anglaise*. Trans. Barbara Bray. New York: Pantheon, 1987. Paris: Editions Gallimard, 1967.

————. *L'Amour*. Paris: Editions Gallimard, 1972.

————. *Blue Eyes, Black Hair*. Trans. Barbara Bray. New York: Pantheon, 1987. Originally published as *Les yeux bleus, cheveux noirs*. Paris: Minuit, 1987.

————. *Destroy, She Said*. Trans. Barbara Bray. New York: Grove Press, 1970. Originally published as *Détruire dit-elle*. Paris: Minuit, 1969.

————. "Dispossessed: An Interview with Marguerite Duras." Trans. Edith Cohen. In *Marguerite Duras*. San Francisco: City Lights Books, 1987.

————. *India Song*. Trans. Barbara Bray. New York: Grove Press, 1976. Originally published as *India Song: Texte-théâtre-film*. Paris: Editions Gallimard, 1973.

————. *The Lover*. Trans. Barbara Bray. New York: Pantheon, 1985. Originally published as *L'Amant*. Paris: Minuit, 1984.

————. *Marguerite Duras*. Trans. Edith Cohen. San Francisco: City Lights Books, 1987. Paris: Albatros, 1976; revised second edition published in *Collection Ça/Cinéma* 2, Paris: Albatros, 1979.

————. *The Ravishing of Lol Stein*. Trans. Richard Seaver. New York: Grove Press, 1966. Originally published as *Le ravissement de Lol V. Stein*. Paris: Editions Gallimard, 1964.

————. *The Vice-Consul*. Trans. Eileen Ellenbogen. New York: Pantheon, 1987. Originally published as *Le vice-consul*. Paris: Editions Gallimard, 1966.

Duras, Marguerite, and Xavière Gauthier. *Woman to Woman*. Trans. Katharine A. Jensen. Lincoln: University of Nebraska Press, 1987. Originally published as *Les parleuses*. Paris: Minuit, 1974.

Duras, Marguerite, and Michelle Porte. *Les lieux de Marguerite Duras*. Paris: Minuit, 1977.

Eisenberg, Nora. "Virginia Woolf's Last Word on Words: *Between the Acts* and 'Anon.'" In *New Feminist Essays on Virginia Woolf*. Ed. Jane Marcus. Lincoln: University of Nebraska Press, 1981.

Evans, Martha Noel. *Masks of Tradition: Women and the Politics of Writing in Twentieth Century France*. Ithaca: Cornell University Press, 1987.

Field, Andrew. *Djuna: The Life and Times of Djuna Barnes*. New York: G. P. Putman's Sons, 1983.

Foster, Hal. *The Anti-Aesthetic: Essays on Postmodern Culture*. Port Townsend, Washington: Bay Press, 1983.

————. *Recodings: Art, Spectacle, Cultural Politics*. Port Townsend, Washington: Bay Press, 1985.

Foucault, Michel. *Discipline and Punish: The Birth of the Prison*. Trans. Alan Sheridan. New York: Vintage, 1977. Originally published as *Surveiller et punir; naissance de la prison*. Paris: Editions Gallimard, 1975.

————. "The Discourse on Language." In *The Archeology of Knowledge*. New York: Pantheon, 1972. Originally published as *L'Ordre du discours*. Paris: Editions Gallimard, 1971.

————. *The History of Sexuality. Vol. 1: An Introduction*. Trans. Robert Hurley. New York: Vintage, 1980. Originally published as *La volenté de savoir*. Paris: Editions Gallimard, 1976.

Freedman, Ralph. *The Lyrical Novel: Studies in Hermann Hesse, André Gide, and Virginia Woolf*. Princeton: Princeton University Press, 1963.

Freud, Sigmund. "On Narcissism: An Introduction." In *The Standard Edition of the Complete Psychological Works*. Ed. James Strachey. London: Hogarth Press, 1953.

Gallop, Jane. *The Daughter's Seduction: Feminism and Psychoanalysis*. Ithaca: Cornell University Press, 1982.

Gilbert, Sandra. "Costumes of the Mind: Transvestism as Metaphor in Modern Literature." *Critical Inquiry* 7 (1980): 391–418.

Gilbert, Sandra, and Susan Gubar. *No Man's Land: The Place of the Woman Writer in the Twentieth Century*, vol. 1. New Haven: Yale University Press, 1987.

Gordon, Lyndall. *Virginia Woolf: A Writer's Life*. Oxford: Oxford University Press, 1984.

Gubar, Susan. "Blessings in Disguise: Cross-Dressing as Re-Dressing for Female Modernists." *Massachusetts Review* 22 (1981): 477–508.

Haller, Evelyn. "Isis Unveiled: Virginia Woolf's Use of Egyptian Myth." In *Virginia Woolf: A Feminist Slant*. Ed. Jane Marcus. Lincoln: University of Nebraska Press, 1983.

Heilbrun, Carolyn. "Sacrificed to Art." Review of *Nora: The Real Life of Molly Bloom* by Brenda Maddox. *Women's Review of Books* 12 (1988): 5.

Husserl-Kapit, Susan. "An Interview with Marguerite Duras." *Signs* 1 (1975): 423–434.

Hutcheon, Linda. *The Politics of Postmodernism*. London: Routledge, 1989.

Irigaray, Luce. *This Sex Which Is Not One*. Ithaca: Cornell University Press, 1985. Originally published as *Ce sexe qui n'en est pas un*. Paris: Minuit, 1977.

Jardine, Alice. *Gynesis: Configurations of Woman and Modernity*. Ithaca: Cornell University Press, 1985.

Johnston, Judith. "The Remediable Flaw: Revisioning Cultural History in *Between the Acts*." In *Virginia Woolf and Bloomsbury: A Centenary*

Celebration. Ed. Jane Marcus. Bloomington: Indiana University Press, 1987.

Kannenstine, Louis. *The Art of Djuna Barnes: Duality and Damnation*. New York: New York University Press, 1977.

Knapp, Bettina. *Anaïs Nin*. New York: Ungar, 1978.

Kofman, Sara. *The Enigma of Woman*. Trans. Catherine Porter. Ithaca: Cornell University Press, 1985. Originally published as *L'Enigme de la femme: La femme dans les textes de Freud*. Paris: Editions Galilée, 1980.

Kristeva, Julia. "The Pain of Sorrow in the Modern World: The Works of Marguerite Duras." *PMLA* 102 (March 1987): 138–152.

———. *Powers of Horror: An Essay on Abjection*. Trans. Leon S. Roudiez. New York: Columbia University Press, 1982. Originally published as *Pouvoirs de l'horreur*. Paris: Editions du Seuil, 1980.

———. *Revolution in Poetic Language*. Trans. Margaret Waller. New York: Columbia University Press, 1984. Originally published as *La révolution du langage poétique*. Paris: Editions du Seuil, 1974.

Lacan, Jacques. *Ecrits: A Selection*. Trans. Alan Sheridan. New York: Norton, 1977. Paris: Editions du Seuil, 1966.

———. *Feminine Sexuality: Jacques Lacan and the Ecole Freudienne*. Trans. Jacqueline Rose. Ed. Juliet Mitchell and Jacqueline Rose. New York: Norton, 1982.

———. *The Four Fundamental Concepts of Psychoanalysis*. Ed. Jacques-Alain Miller. Trans. Alan Sheridan. New York: Norton, 1978. Originally published as "Les quatre concepts fondamentaux de la psychanalyse" in *Le séminaire de Jacques Lacan, Livre XI*. Paris: Editions du Seuil, 1973.

———. "Homage to Marguerite Duras, on *Le ravissement de Lol V. Stein*." Trans. Peter Connor. In *Marguerite Duras*. San Francisco: City Lights Books, 1987.

Lanser, Susan Sniader. "Speaking in Tongues: *Ladies Almanack* and the Language of Celebration." *Frontiers: A Journal of Women's Studies* 4 (1979): 39–46.

Lawrence, D. H. *The Rainbow*. New York: Penguin, 1976.

———. *Women in Love*. New York: Penguin, 1976.

Lentricchia, Frank. *Ariel and the Police*. Madison: University of Wisconsin Press, 1988.

Little, Judy. "Festive Comedy in Woolf's *Between the Acts*." *Women and Literature* (Spring 1977): 26–37.

Lydon, Mary. "Translating Duras: 'The Seated Man in the Passage.'" *Contemporary Literature* 24 (1983): 259–275.

Lyon, Elisabeth. "The Cinema of Lol V. Stein." *Camera Obscura* 6 (1980): 9–39.

Macciocchi, Maria-Antonietta. "Female Sexuality in Fascist Ideology." *Feminist Review* 1 (1975): 75.

Marcus, Jane. "Carnival of the Animals." *Women's Review of Books* 8 (1984): 6–7.

———. "Laughing at Leviticus: *Nightwood* as Woman's Circus Epic." In *Silence and Power: Djuna Barnes: A Reevaluation.* Ed. Mary Lynn Broe. Carbondale: Southern Illinois University Press, 1991.

———. "Liberty, Sorority, Misogyny." In *Virginia Woolf and the Languages of Patriarchy.* Ed. Jane Marcus. Bloomington: Indiana University Press, 1987. Originally published in *Representation of Women in Fiction.* Ed. Carolyn Heilbrun and Margaret Higonnet. Baltimore: Johns Hopkins University Press, 1983.

———. "Thinking Back through Our Mothers." In *New Feminist Essays on Virginia Woolf.* Ed. Jane Marcus. Lincoln: University of Nebraska Press, 1981.

Marini, Marcelle. *Territoires du féminin avec Marguerite Duras.* Paris: Minuit, 1977.

Messerli, Douglas. *Djuna Barnes Interviews.* Washington, D.C.: Sun and Moon Press, 1985.

Miller, Alice. *Thou Shalt Not Be Aware: Society's Betrayal of the Child.* New York: Farrar, Straus, Giroux, 1984.

Minow-Pinkney, Makiko. *Virginia Woolf and the Problem of the Subject.* Sussex: Harvester Press, 1987.

Moi, Toril. *Sexual/Textual Politics: Feminist Literary Theory.* London: Methuen, 1985.

Montrelay, Michele. *L'ombre et le nom.* Paris: Minuit, 1977.

Moore, Madeline. *The Short Season between Two Silences: The Mystical and the Political in the Novels of Virginia Woolf.* Boston: Allen and Unwin, 1984.

Murphy, Carol. *Alienation and Absence in the Novels of Marguerite Duras.* Lexington: French Forum, 1982.

Naremore, James. *The World without a Self.* New Haven: Yale University Press, 1973.

New Larousse Encyclopedia of Myth. London: Hamlyn, 1968.

Rabant, Christiane. "La bête chanteuse." *L'Arc* 58 (1974).

Rivette, Jacques, and Jean Narboni. "An Interview with Marguerite Duras." Trans. Helen Lane Cumberford. In *Destroy, She Said.* New York: Grove Press, 1970.

Rose, Phyllis. *Woman of Letters: A Life of Virginia Woolf.* New York: Harcourt Brace Jovanovich, 1978.

Roseman, Ellen Bayuk. *The Invisible Presence: Virginia Woolf and the Mother-Daughter Relationship.* Baton Rouge: Louisiana State University Press, 1986.

Scarry, Elaine. *The Body in Pain: The Making and Unmaking of the World.* New York: Oxford University Press, 1985.

Scott, James. *Djuna Barnes*. Boston: Twayne Publishers, 1976.

Sears, Sallie. "Theater of War: Virginia Woolf's *Between the Acts*." In *Virginia Woolf: A Feminist Slant*. Ed. Jane Marcus. Lincoln: University of Nebraska Press, 1983.

 Showalter, Elaine. *A Literature of Their Own: British Women Novelists from Brontë to Lessing*. Princeton: Princeton University Press, 1977.

Solomon, Barbara Probst. "Marguerite Duras: The Politics of Passion." *Partisan Review* 54 (1987): 415–422.

Spivak, Gayatri C. "Unmaking and Making in *To the Lighthouse*." In *Women and Language in Literature and Society*. Ed. Sally McConnell-Ginet, Ruth Borker, and Nelly Furman. New York: Praeger, 1980.

Stevens, Wallace. *The Collected Poems*. New York: Vintage, 1982.

Transue, Pamela. *Virginia Woolf and the Politics of Style*. Albany: State University of New York Press, 1986.

Van Wert, William F. "The Cinema of Marguerite Duras: Sound and Voice in a Closed Room." *Film Quarterly* 33 (1979): 22–29.

Wallis, Brian, ed. *Art after Modernism: Rethinking Representation*. New York: The Museum of Contemporary Art, 1984.

Waugh, Patricia. *Feminine Fictions: Revisiting the Postmodern*. London: Routledge, 1989.

Willis, Sharon. *Marguerite Duras: Writing on the Body*. Urbana: University of Illinois Press, 1987.

Woodhull, Winifred. "Marguerite Duras and the Question of Community." *Modern Language Studies* 17 (Winter 1987): 3–16.

Woolf, Leonard. *Downhill All the Way: An Autobiography of the Years 1919–1939*. London: Hogarth, 1970.

Woolf, Virginia. *Between the Acts*. London: Hogarth, 1969.

———. *The Diaries of Virginia Woolf*. Ed. Anne Olivier Bell with Andrew McNeillie. 5 vols. London: Hogarth, 1977–1984.

———. *The Letters of Virginia Woolf*. Ed. Nigel Nicolson with Joanne Trautmann. 6 vols. London: Hogarth, 1975–1980.

———. *Moments of Being: Unpublished Autobiographical Writings*. Ed. Jeanne Schulkind. Sussex: University Press, 1985.

———. *Mrs. Dalloway*. New York: Harcourt Brace Jovanovich, 1953.

———. *Pointz Hall*. Ed. Mitchell A. Leaska. New York: University Publications, 1983.

———. "A Sketch of the Past." In *Moments of Being: Unpublished Autobiographical Writings*. Sussex: University Press, 1985.

———. *To the Lighthouse*. London: Hogarth, 1967.

———. "22 Hyde Park Gate." In *Moments of Being: Unpublished Autobiographical Writings*. Sussex: University Press, 1985.

———. *The Waves*. London: Hogarth, 1972.

————. *A Writer's Diary*. Ed. Leonard Woolf. New York: Harcourt Brace Jovanovich, 1953.

————. *Women and Writing*. Ed. Michelle Barrett. New York: Harcourt Brace Jovanovich, 1979.

Zwerdling, Alex. *Virginia Woolf and the Real World*. Berkeley: University of California Press, 1986.

Index